D0695719

CELEBRATING LOVE

His Holiness
Sri Sri Ravi Shankar

Weekly Knowledge
through 2002

Edited by
Bill Hayden and Anne Elixhauser

CELEBRATING LOVE

BY

HIS HOLINESS
SRI SRI RAVI SHANKAR

Copyright 2005

All rights reserved

First edition published August 2006

Printed in India

Printed in India by Jwalamukhi Mudranalaya Pvt. Ltd., Bangalore
Ph: +91-80-26601064, 26617243

No part of this book may be reproduced or transmitted in any form or by any means, electronic or mechanical, including photocopying, recording, or any information storage or retrieval system without prior permission in writing from the publisher.

Compiled and Edited by
Bill Hayden and Anne Elixhauser
Editing and Production Support by Laura Weinberg

ISBN 978-938011403-6

Published by :
Sri Sri Publications Trust
Art of Living International Center
21st km, Kanakapura Road, Udaypura
Bangalore – 560082, Phone: 080 32722473
email: info@srisripublications.com
www.artoflivingshop.com

In 1995 His Holiness Sri Sri Ravi Shankar began a weekly tradition of creating a short talk for people seeking inspiration, wisdom or solutions to their challenges. Each week this knowledge flowed to every continent, and each year these talks were compiled into a volume called "An Intimate Note to the Sincere Seeker." In 2001 "Celebrating Silence" organized most of the first five years of weekly knowledge into one book. On September 5, 2002, Sri Sri distributed his last weekly knowledge ending a series of 365 notes of wisdom. This companion edition to "Celebrating Silence" collects the last two years of talks, including some notes that had been left out of "Celebrating Silence."

Those who were fortunate to be with Sri Sri when a weekly knowledge was created found the wisdom enlightening and the discussions sparkling with joy and insight. He once said, "In the presence of your satguru, knowledge flourishes, sorrow diminishes, and without any reason, joy wells up and all talents manifest." Today these notes continue to cause the same experiences, and when someone seeking wisdom or advice randomly opens a volume they often find exactly what they require – as if the paradigm of time and separateness was replaced by a timeless continuum of caring and intelligent consciousness.

The journey for these weekly essays began in Big Sur, California and ended in New Delhi, India – a giant seven-year circle drew to a close. The voyage included many passages around the world, during which the hearts and minds of millions were blessed with the wisdom of this extraordinary man.

For Anne and I, this also brings to closure the 7 years we facilitated the weekly knowledge. We continue to miss them, but the process of re-reading and studying these compact gems reminds us again and again how much this knowledge can guide us through tough times and through growth times – it just takes sincerity and an open mind.

Like "Celebrating Silence," this collection is thematic rather than chronological. The first chapter helps us understand the more concrete issues that we deal with, such as worry, anger and violence – those things we want to change, as well as those things we want to culture such as love and dispassion. The second chapter, building on the first, teaches us what it means to be on a spiritual path, discussing service, surrender, human values and having a spiritual guide. The third chapter is the culmination, with wisdom for understanding God, our relationship to Him, and to our inner Self – that which we sincerely seek, often without knowing, leading us to celebrate in love.

His Holiness
Sri Sri Ravi Shankar

When love glows, it is bliss
When it flows, it is compassion
When it blows, it is anger
When it ferments, it is jealousy
When it is all "no's," it is hatred
When it acts, it is perfection
When love knows, it is me.

Sri Sri

Chapter One

The You That You Want to Change

To love someone whom you like is insignificant.
To love someone because they love you is of no consequence.

To love someone whom you do not like means you have learned a lesson in life.

To love someone who blames you for no reason shows that you have learned the art of living.

In the air from Singapore to Hawaii
April 12, 2001

Learning is inevitable. By doing things right you learn and by doing things wrong you also learn. From every situation, from everybody, you learn either what to do or what not to do. Either by making mistakes or by doing things correctly, you can only learn. Learning is inevitable.

It is only when you sleep that you do not learn. And if you are asleep in your life, there is neither pain nor pleasure nor learning. Most people are in such deep slumber. That is why many people do not even make an effort to get out of their pain.

Washington, D.C., United States
July 2, 2002

Mistakes happen all the time. Often you get irritated by mistakes and you want to correct them, but how many can you correct? You correct others' mistakes for two reasons. The first is when someone's mistake bothers you, and the second is when you correct someone for their own sake so they can grow, not because it bothers you. Correcting mistakes for the first reason – when the mistake bothers you – does not work.

To correct mistakes you need both authority and love. Authority and love seem to be contradictory but in reality they are not. Authority without love is stifling and does not work. Love without authority is shallow. You need both but they need to be in the right combination so you can be successful in correcting others' mistakes. This can happen if you are totally dispassionate and centered.

When you allow room for mistakes, you can be both authoritative and sweet. That is how the Divine is – the right balance of both. Krishna and Jesus had both. People in love also exercise authority with those they love. Authority and love exist in all relationships.

Lake Tahoe, California, United States
July 12, 2001

Do not tell a person about a mistake he knows that he made. What is the use of pointing out a mistake that he knows he has committed? By doing this, you will only make that person feel more guilty, defensive, or resentful and this only creates more distance. And do not point out a person's mistake if he is aware of it but does not want you to know about it. Often people know their mistakes, but they do not want you to point them out.

You should only point out a person's mistake if he is not aware of it and wants to know about it.

Think about the usefulness of your comments. Before pointing out a person's mistake, see whether your comments will help to improve the situation, foster love, or bring harmony. A magnanimous person does not point out the mistakes of others and make them feel guilty. Instead, they correct others' mistakes with compassion and care, not through words but through their attitude.

New York City, New York, United States
August 29, 2000

Often, in establishing your righteousness, you are insensitive to the feelings of others. When someone is hurt, arguing with them and establishing your righteousness will be in vain. By simply saying "I'm sorry," you can uplift the other person and take away the bitterness. In many situations saying "I'm sorry" is better than establishing your righteousness – it can avert much unpleasantness.

Sorry – this one word of five letters, when said sincerely, can remove anger, guilt, hatred and distance.

Many people feel pride in hearing "I'm sorry" from others – it boosts their ego. But when you say "I'm sorry" to a wise man, it evokes compassion at your ignorance. And when you say "I'm sorry" to your Guru, he will get angry and say, "Go! Listen to Ashtavakra!"* Your apology indicates doership – you feel that *you* have made a mistake.

A mistake is part of an unconscious mind. An unconscious mind cannot do right while a conscious mind can do no wrong. The mind that makes the mistake and the mind that realizes the mistake – the mind that says "I'm sorry" – are entirely different, aren't they? The mind that apologies cannot be an unconscious mind. Therefore, sincerely saying "I'm sorry" is a big mistake.

Did you get it or are you confused? If you did not get it, do not feel sorry or … you can feel sorry!

How strange – truth is paradoxical!

European Ashram, Bad Antogast, Germany
December 28, 2000

* The Ashtavakra Gita commentary by Sri Sri where he elaborates on the conversation between the saint Ashtavakra and King Janaka.

Your body is like a washing machine, your mind is like your clothing, each lifetime is like one washing cycle, pure water is like love, and knowledge is the detergent. The mind enters the body to get cleansed and purified.

But if instead of detergent you use dirt, then you have dirty clothes, dirtier than before. You will have to continue putting clothes in the washing machine to get them cleaned. And the process repeats again and again. Similarly, you will have many more births until you stop repeating the mistakes that you have made.

Gyan Mandir, Bangalore, India
December 21, 1995

Fights can only happen among equals. When you fight with someone, you make that person your equal. But in reality there is no one at par with you. When you keep people either above you or below you, there is no fight. When people are above you, you respect them. When they are below you, you love them and feel compassionate. Either submission or compassion can quickly stop a fight. This is something to consider when you are tired of fighting. But when you are well rested, just fight and have fun.

The same is true of the mind. When the mind is caught up in the senses or thinks it is equal to the senses, there is constant conflict. But when the mind is smaller than the senses, as in animals, there is no conflict. And when the mind realizes that it is bigger than the senses, again there is no conflict. When the mind transcends the senses, it comes back to its true nature, which is innocence – "in no sense."

Does this make sense?

Bangalore Ashram, India
August 18, 2000

Your inability to do something, such as break a habit, can cause a pinch. When you are deeply pained by something, then that will rid you of that habit. If you are pained by your shortcomings, then you are a sadhak.* Pain pushes you out of addiction.

Los Angeles, California, United States
January 30, 1997

* a spiritual seeker

If you observe your behavior, you will notice that you procrastinate when doing something good but hurry when it comes to doing something bad. For example, if you are angry, you want to express it immediately.

Do you know why? Because virtues are your very nature and will never leave you while your vices are not your nature and they will leave you. Negative tendencies are transient and will leave you if you do not act on them immediately. Frustration and crying cannot stay long, especially with the same intensity. Perhaps you are concerned that your vices will leave you if you do not act on them.

It is wise to postpone acting on vices, for they will not stay, and to act immediately to do good; otherwise, you will continue to postpone doing good for the next few lifetimes!

Bangalore Ashram, India
February 8, 2002

Why do people hunger for power?

People crave power because they want attention and recognition. Power is a means, just like money. Their passion is for the goal. People who see power or money as an end in itself do not live, they simply exist.

If you do not realize that you are the power – that you are enlightened – then you crave power.

If you do not have talents, love, or passion, or if you are not innocent and childlike, then you will crave attention and recognition. Just as some politicians, you will crave power. If you have no talents and you are not contributing substantially to society such as an artist, a scientist, an Art of Living teacher, or a volunteer – then you will hunger for power. If you do not have a love or a passion to help transform society, then you will hunger for power.

If you are not innocent and childlike and do not have a sense of belongingness with the whole world, then you will hunger for power.

True power is the power of the spirit. Real confidence, strength and happiness all spring from the spirit. The one who knows this and has this will not crave power at all.

Bangalore Ashram, India
August 30, 2001

Ambition indicates a lack of self-confidence. When you know you can achieve something easily, you will not be ambitious; you will simply be confident about it. Your ambition indicates challenge and uncertainty, which is contrary to self-confidence. So one who has total self-confidence cannot be ambitious, nor can a person who totally lacks confidence. For ambition to be present, you must have a small amount of confidence and total ignorance of the Self. It is nearly impossible to have total confidence without Self-knowledge.

People take pride in being ambitious. The wise man will only smile at them. You can never be ambitious about something you know you can achieve effortlessly. You can only be ambitious about something that requires effort, that poses a challenge, and that you cannot be certain you will achieve. Ambition takes away the joy of the moment.

With the knowledge of the Self, there is nothing left to achieve for the entire nature of existence is mere play and display of your own consciousness.

With Self-knowledge nothing is challenging to you, nor do you need to make an effort. Nature is ready to fulfill your intentions even before they arise, giving you no chance to crave or desire. Nature does not allow the wise to have desires or ambition, nor does it allow the unwise to fulfill their desires or ambitions, or to discard them.

Hawaii, United States
April 17, 2001

Nature has built a little fear into all living beings. This fear makes life defend itself, protect itself. Like salt in food, a little fear is essential for people to be righteous.

- Fear of hurting someone makes you more conscious.
- Fear of failure makes you more keen and dynamic.
- Fear moves you from carelessness to taking care.
- Fear moves you from being insensitive to being sensitive.
- Fear moves you from dullness to alertness.

Total lack of fear may lead to destructive tendencies – a distorted ego knows no fear. Nor does one with expanded consciousness. While the ego dismisses fear and acts in a destructive manner, the wise one acknowledges fear and takes refuge in the Divine.

When you are in love, when you are surrendered, there is no fear. Ego, too, knows no fear. But there is a difference – like the difference between heaven and earth – between these two types of fearless states.

Fear makes you righteous; fear brings you close to surrender; fear keeps you on the path; fear keeps you from being destructive. Peace and law are maintained on the planet because of fear.

A newborn child knows no fear – the baby relies totally on its mother. When a child, a kitten, or a bird start becoming independent, they experience fear and this makes them run back to their mothers. This is inbuilt by nature to sustain life.

So, the purpose of fear is to bring you back to the source.

Udaipur, Jagmandir, India
March 1, 2001

At the present time, many are anxious about how to deal with their anxiety. Here are some of the ways you can manage anxiety.

- Sing, dance and celebrate. The very intention to celebrate will pull you to a more harmonious state.
- Think about what you can do for others rather than thinking about yourself. Get energized through service.
- Have an attitude of sacrifice.
- Remind yourself that you are committed to a greater goal.
- Practice yoga, breathing and meditation.
- Know the impermanence of the world.
- Have faith in and surrender to the Divine. Know that there is a supreme power who loves you, is behind you and a accepts you totally. Feeling secure comes with this sense of belongingness.
- Be courageous and invoke the lion within you.
- Be unpredictable for a while. Anxiety always relates to some anticipated action so do something completely irrelevant and unpredictable.
- Be ready to face the worst. This will leave you with stability in your mind.
- Remember a similar situation in the past when you were able to overcome your anxiety.

Montreal Ashram, Canada
October 4, 2001

When someone blames you, you feel a heavy load, and when you talk about it, the unpleasant feeling is spread to all around you. At that moment wake up and see you are Being and nothing can touch you. This is all just a drama which you have created. You have gone through this over and over again. All the accusations you face in your life are your own creation. Knowing this, you will feel free and light.

Taking responsibility for all the experiences in life makes you powerful and will put an end to grumbling, retribution, explanations and a host of other negative tendencies. Taking full responsibility makes you free.

When someone blames you, directly or indirectly, what do you do?

- Do you register it in your mind and get emotionally upset?
- Do you dismiss it altogether without taking a lesson from it?
- Do you talk about it with people, wasting everyone's time?
- Do you pity yourself and blame your shortcomings?
- Do you blame the other person?
- Do you generalize and eternalize the problem?

When this happens, you are not living up to this knowledge. You need to do the Art of Living introductory course at least six times and read all the weekly knowledge.

However, if you:

- Laugh at it and not even take notice,
- Treat it as a non-event, not even worth talking about or taking any action,
- Treat opinions and accusations as passing clouds and more of an entertainment,
- Discourage dwelling on unpleasant and negative moments,
- Are non-judgmental and absolutely unshaken in your space of love,
- Remain centered and calm, and do not take pride in your growth or wisdom,

Then you are a pride to your tutor – the master.

In the air from Singapore to Hawaii
April 12, 2001

The head worries and the heart feels. The two cannot function at the same time; when your feelings dominate, worry dissolves.

If you worry a lot, your feelings die and you become stuck in your head. Worrying makes your mind and heart inert and dull; it steals your energy and prevents you from thinking clearly. Worries entangle you; they trap you in a cage. Worries are uncertain since they are about the future.

When you feel, you do not worry. Feelings are like flowers – they come up, they blossom and they die. Feelings rise, they fall and then disappear. When your feelings are expressed, you are relieved. When you become angry, you express your anger and the next moment you feel fine. Or when you are upset, you cry and you get over it. Feelings last for some short time and then they drop away, but worry eats at you much longer and eventually consumes you.

Feelings make you spontaneous. Children feel, so they are spontaneous, but adults put brakes on their feelings and start worrying. Worry obstructs action, while feelings propel action. Worrying about negative feelings is a blessing because it puts brakes on those feelings, preventing you from acting on them. But we usually do not worry about positive feelings. Though, when you think you are feeling too much, then you often start worrying about your feelings.

Offering your worries is prayer and prayer moves you in feelings.

Montreal Ashram, Canada
July 19, 2001

Why do you feel awkward? How do you stop feeling awkward?

If you have always been the center of attention and are suddenly sidelined, you may feel out of place. Similarly if you have always been on the sidelines and are suddenly pushed to center stage, you may experience restlessness. A very busy person with nothing to do, or a laidback person who is faced with responsibilities, may also experience restlessness. If you are accustomed to ordering others around and suddenly have to take orders, or if you usually follow orders and then are made to give them, you may feel out of place. Feeling out of place can block reason and distort logic.

If the situation you are in is inevitable, tolerate it. If it is avoidable, walk away from it. If you feel that it can expand your abilities, smile through it.

Love something about an awkward situation. This will increase your comfort zone. When your comfort zone increases, no one will be able to push your buttons and you will become centered and unshakable. Every awkward situation is a test for how deep you are in the knowledge.

New Delhi, India
March 4, 2002

Rage has no ears, nor does it have vision.
It only leads to reaction.
And reaction leads to regret.
Regret causes frustration.
Frustration clouds reason.
Unreasonable acts provoke rage, starting a vicious cycle.

Only self-knowledge and devotion can free you from this vicious cycle. In the fire of knowledge, when rage and revenge are offered, the warmth of the blemish-free Self shines forth. This is the true Yagya.

Rishikesh, India
March 6, 2002

Many people have a problem letting go of control, causing anxiety, restlessness and soured relationships.

Wake up and see – are you really ever in control? What do you control? Perhaps a tiny part of your waking state! You are not in control when you are sleeping or dreaming. You are not in control of the thoughts and emotions coming to you. You may choose to express them or not, but they come to you without your permission. Most of the functions of your body are not under your control. Do you think you are in control of all the events in your life, in the world, or in the universe? That is a joke! When you look at things from this angle, you need not be afraid of losing control, because you have none to lose.

Whether you realize it or not, only when you truly relax can you let go of your sense of control. Your identification with being somebody does not let you totally relax and it limits your domain.

European Ashram, Bad Antogast, Germany
December 27, 2001

Unfortunate are those who crave for the world.
Fortunate are those who crave for the Divine.
Unwise are those who make you crave for the world.
Wise are those who make you crave for the Divine.

The source of conflict is the notion of "mine" and "yours." Self-knowledge eases the sense of limited belongingness and resolves this conflict. When knowledge dawns in you, there is no stranger in the whole world. At the same time you realize that you know very little about even your nearest one. You cannot understand anyone totally for life is a mystery! Wake up and see. All these distinctions – "Me, Mine, Others" – simply dissolve.

Ottawa, Canada
September 8, 2000

Today is Krishna's birthday. Krishna's life was full of conflicts and yet he kept smiling and dancing. May you dance through the conflicts and contribute to this planet.

Bangalore Ashram, India
September 5, 1996

The worst act of reason is war.

Every war has a reason, and the reason justifies the war. Those who engage in war reason it out. But reason is limited. As reason changes, the justification falls apart. All the reasons for every war appear to be justifiable to some limited minds and for a limited time. Hence, war becomes inevitable on this planet.

Only human beings wage war. No other species in creation engages in war or mass destruction, as they have no reason to do so. Animals take their prey and let everything else just be. But mankind, from time immemorial, has engaged in war because man bases his actions on reason. Man gives a reason to every act of his and justifies it. But as reasons change, his justifications fall apart.

Man must transcend reason – only then can he realize Divinity and will not engage in war. Only when people become sensible, rise above hatred and have heightened consciousness, can war be stopped.

Kolkata, India
September 20, 2001

The act which is only destructive and inflicts suffering on both oneself and others is terrorism. In such an act human values are lost in the process of achieving a goal.

Some of the factors that lead to terrorism are frustration and desperation in achieving a goal, impulsive action, shortsightedness and confused emotions. Terrorism can also stem from having a non-verifiable concept of heaven and merit, and a childish concept of God where God favors some and is angry with others, undermining the Divine's omniscience and omnipotence.

Terrorism induces a psychosis of fear in everyone, and it increases poverty, suffering, and loss of life with no apparent gain. Instead of life-supporting solutions, the terrorist chooses destruction as an answer. If you criticize without giving a solution, know that it comes from the seed of terrorism.

Although there are certain qualities you can appreciate in a terrorist such as fearlessness, commitment to a goal and sacrifice, you must learn from them things that you should never do – valuing ideas and concepts more than life, having a narrow perspective of life and dishonoring life's diversity.

The remedy for terrorism is to:

- Inculcate a broader perspective of life.
- Value life more than race, religion and nationality.
- Provide education in human values – friendliness, compassion, cooperation and upliftment.
- Teach methods to release stress and tension.
- Cultivate confidence in achieving noble aims by peaceful and nonviolent means.
- Weed out destructive tendencies with spiritual upliftment.

Question: Can terrorism be more than physical violence, such as cultural or economic terrorism?

Yes. The solution for economic violence is to "Think globally, buy locally," and the solution for cultural violence is to "Broaden your vision, deepen your roots."

Question: How does one cope with the aftermath of terrorism?

Faith and prayer. When disaster happens, anger is inevitable. To take precautions that you not react improperly, wisdom is needed and not emotional outbursts. One mistake cannot be corrected by another mistake. Strive to foster multicultural and multi-religious education and spiritual upliftment in every part of the globe, for the world will not be safe if even a small pocket of people are left in ignorance.

European Ashram, Bad Antogast, Germany
September 28, 2001

Violence and nonviolence do not depend on an act but on the intention behind it. The basis of violence is anger, lust, hatred, jealousy, greed, frustration and aggression.

A surgeon cuts open a person's belly; so does a criminal. The action is similar but the surgeon's intention is to save life and the criminal's is to destroy it. Violence or nonviolence is determined by the attitude and not by the act.

Even a war can be nonviolent if it is devoid of anger, hatred, jealousy, or greed and if its intent is to educate those who cannot be educated in any other way. Even charity can be an act of violence if it takes away self-esteem and inflicts slavery. A war can be an act of compassion if it helps to establish the right perspective.

Bangalore Ashram, India
October 11, 2001

Today is Deepawali, the festival of lights. There are many stories associated with this day.

It was on this day that the demon Narakasura was killed. King Narakasura – Naraka means hell – had been granted a boon that he could only be destroyed by a woman. Lord Krishna's wife, Satyabhama, was the one to destroy him.

Why could only Satyabhama kill Naraka? Satya means truth and bhama means the beloved. Untruth or lack of love cannot conquer hell. It cannot be removed by aggression. Hell can only be erased by love and surrender. Non-aggression, love and surrender are the inherent qualities of a woman. Hence only Satyabhama, the true beloved, could remove hell and bring the light back. And Narakasura's last wish was that every house should celebrate his demise with lights to mark the end of darkness. This is Deepawali.

It was also today that Lord Rama returned to Ayodhya, his kingdom, after his victory over Ravana, the demon king. Ayodhya means that which cannot be destroyed, or life. Ram means the Atma – the Self. When the Self rules in life, then knowledge lights up. There is life everywhere. But when the spirit is awakened in life, Deepawali happens.

Bangalore Ashram, India
October 26, 2000

The inability to experience joy and sorrow is inertia.

- Experiencing joy and sorrow is a trait of consciousness.
- Being happy in one's own joy and sad in one's own sorrow is a trait of animals.
- Being happy at another's joy and saddened by another's sorrow is a trait of humans.
- If you are saddened by another's sorrow, then sorrow will never come to you.
- If you are happy at another's joy, then joy will never leave you.
- Seeing that every relative joy is also a misery is a sign of dispassion.
- And seeing both joy and sorrow as just a technique is a sign of the wise.
- To consider sorrow mere illusion is divinity.
- Transcending joy and sorrow and being established in the Self is perfection.

As the late Swami Sharanananda said, "Pray for the strength to serve in joy and to sacrifice in sorrow."

Bangalore Ashram, India
May 31, 2001

The best solution to a problem is not to have the problem at all. The second best solution is to willingly accept the problem and see it as a challenge. The third best solution is to know that the problem is just a monster under the bed – it is not real.

The final solution is to know that nature provides you the solution even before giving you the problem. First you met me and then you had a problem! There are no bacteria in the winter since herbs to heal you do not grow then. In the spring, the herbs grow first and then the bugs arrive. In the summer, the shade comes before the summer sun gets strong. So, nature takes good care of you.

Question: What if longing is a problem?

Longing ripens you. Do not solve all your problems. Keep at least one of them. You need something to munch on – and life goes on.

European Ashram, Bad Antogast, Germany
August 24, 2000

Whenever there is a problem, you either deny it saying there is no problem, or you sit down to solve the problem and make it a big issue. Neither of these help. A problem does not disappear when you deny it and it does not get solved when you sit down to solve it.

The five steps to solve a problem are:

- Admit it exists.
- See it as a small problem and do not say it is big.
- If it concerns people, keep in touch with them instead of avoiding them.
- Talk less and give time a chance.
- Get together and celebrate. When you celebrate and put the problem on the back burner, you will see that the problem gets solved in time.

So it is wise not to sit down to solve a problem. Many of the meetings to solve problems end up in disaster. If you do not have any problems, you will create problems or you will become a problem yourself! If you have a small problem in your pocket to solve, it will give focus to your mind.

It is better to have a problem than to be a problem.

European Ashram, Bad Antogast, Germany
November 23, 2000

From time to time the earth shakes and in its shaking wakes up the man who is in slumber, the man who not only misuses Nature but puts his faith in bricks and mortar. Your true security is in the Self, not in bricks and mortar. Perhaps this is what Nature wants to convey to you. Earthquakes, floods and volcanoes all drive home the truth that nothing is permanent and you can find no security in that which is impermanent. Disasters come to you as a shock and wake you up.

When such calamities occur, we try to understand their cause so that we can blame someone. Strangely, when you find someone to blame, you feel comfortable, but with natural calamities you cannot blame anyone. They come to you as a shock. With wisdom, shocks can make you grow in leaps and bounds. Without wisdom, a shock can only lead you to negativity and depression.

Question: Why would nature destroy small innocent children?

Nature just does its job. It does not discriminate between young and old. Do you think that all those who eat bamboo shoots and eggs, or who pluck flower buds, are not compassionate? Maybe, maybe not!

Instead of questioning Nature, wake up and see the opportunity for seva, or service. See what is happening in Gujarat now. Today, hundreds and thousands of people are engaged in service activities that would not have happened otherwise. The reconstruction of Gujarat would not be taking place if not for earthquake. Out of the destruction, a fresh water spring has appeared in a region that has been continuously drought prone.

Wisdom is considering the earth as your Valentine. Whether it shakes or breaks, it is dear to you. You always see good coming from it.

The four elements, other than space, create turbulence from time to time. If you depend on them for support, they will shake you and lead you back to space.

Finding security in inner space is spirituality.

Bangalore Ashram, India
February 14, 2001

Being forgetful of your nature is the root cause of all problems and suffering in life. But the very remembrance of your nature, which is godliness, brings freedom. Here memory is your best friend. The purpose of knowledge is to remind you of your true nature. In the Bhagavad Gita, Arjuna said to Krishna, "My memory is back. Now I have realized my true nature and will do as you say."

Memory is a blessing and is your best friend when it helps you realize your true nature. Memory is a hindrance when it does not let you be free of events, pleasant or unpleasant. Pleasant events create cravings and competition in the mind and do not allow fresh experiences. Unpleasant events bias perception and create paranoia. So memory is both a blessing and a hindrance depending on whether you remember your nature or whether you are stuck with events in time and space.

European Ashram, Bad Antogast, Germany
January 4, 2002

Ego is an impediment for a leader, a wise man, a merchant, or a servant, but it is required for a warrior and a competitor.

A warrior takes on challenges and commitments and stands by them.

Ego makes you sacrifice yourself for a cause. Ego gives strength and courage and brings valor to meet challenges with endurance and perseverance. A strong ego will counteract depression. Ego is often considered selfish but it is the greatest motivating factor for creativity and generosity. Ego propels you to venture into the unknown.

There are three types of ego – sattvic, rajasic and tamasic.

- Tamasic ego is barbaric, blind and self-destructive.
- Rajasic ego is self-centered and causes misery to oneself and others.
- Sattvic ego is creative and has protective tendencies.

If you cannot surrender, at least have a sattvic ego, as a sattvic ego is always ready to sacrifice.

Rishikesh, India
March 8, 2001

What really perturbs you? Is it the foolishness that goes on around you?

It is foolish to be perturbed by foolishness. Foolishness cannot overpower or annihilate wisdom nor does foolishness last very long. When you are not well-grounded in wisdom, then foolishness perturbs you, throws you off balance. When you create space for foolishness, you will not get perturbed by it, rather you will laugh and move on. Otherwise you get hateful or angry, or become stressed by foolish acts.

When you know that truth is eternal and invincible, you accept foolishness as a joke and remain unmoved by it. Those who are averse to foolishness or get irritated by it are members of the fools' club.

Austin, Texas, United States
January 11, 2002

A lady came to Sri Sri and said that her husband lied to her. She was very upset.

Sri Sri asked, "Why does your husband lie to you? He lies to you because he loves you and is afraid to lose your love or to hurt you. If he did not love you, he wouldn't lie to you."

New York City, New York, United States
August 29, 2000

Examine the cause of your friendships. Here are the reasons you make friends:

- You have common enemies. Fear or a threat to survival brings people together.
- You have common problems such as an illness or job dissatisfaction.
- You have common job or professional interests.
- You have common tastes and interests, such as sports, movies, music and hobbies.
- You have compassion or provide service.
- You become friends merely because of long-term acquaintance with one another.

Brave are those who nurture friendships for only friendship's sake. Such friendships will never die nor become soured for they are born out of your friendly nature, and only through wisdom can you be friendly by nature.

Jakarta, Java, Indonesia
May 23, 2002

There are two types of respect. The first is respect that comes to you because of your position, fame, or wealth. This type of respect is impermanent. It can be lost once you lose your wealth or status. The second type of respect comes because of your smile and your virtues such as honesty, kindness, commitment and patience. This respect no one can take away.

The less you are attached to your virtues, the more self-respect you have. When you get attached to your virtues, you disdain others and then your virtues start diminishing. Non-attachment to virtues brings the highest self-respect.

Ego is often confused with self-esteem. Ego needs another for comparison, but self-esteem is just confidence in oneself. For example, a gentleman claiming that he is skilled in mathematics or geography has self-esteem. But to say, "I know better than you," is ego.

Ego simply means lack of respect for the Self.

Your ego will often leave you upset, but if you have self-esteem, you will be unshaken by external factors. In self-respect everything is a game, winning or losing has no meaning, every step is joy and every move is celebration. With Self-esteem you simply realize you have it.

Bangalore Ashram, India
December 16, 2001

A sense of belonging can bring about a host of negative behaviors – demands, jealousy, lack of awareness and ingratitude. Just look at your own life. You are nicer to strangers, feel more grateful to them and give them more attention than to the people you feel "belong" to you. A sense of belonging reduces gratefulness and awareness, and gives rise to demands that destroy love. This is the biggest problem in relationships. With a sense of belonging comes a feeling of being carefree and indifferent.

Look...belongingness can make you insensitive and dull, and can remove the charm in life. In any case, who belongs to whom in this world? You are a stranger here and everyone is a stranger to you. Blessed are those who feel they are strangers.

You feel more obligation to a stranger than to a person you feel close to. Obligation is very good at keeping a check on your ego; it makes you humble. There is no greater antidote to ego than humility, and humility is the beginning of all virtues.

People have such resistance to obligations. They do not realize they are always under obligations, whether giving or taking. Dull people think they are obliged only when they take. Wise people know that even when they are giving they are under obligation, as the person has accepted what they give. So whether you give or take, you are under obligations. And if someone does not give or take, they are still under obligation because they are freeing you from visible obligations – you are obliged even to those who do not make you obliged.

Life – you – continually renews itself by becoming a stranger in this old and familiar world. You are simply loaded with obligations and you are a total stranger in this world at every moment.

Sao Paulo, Brazil
April 25, 2001

One of the rarest character combinations is the co-existence of confidence and humility. Often people who are confident are not humble and people with humility are not confident. Confidence blended with humility is most appreciated by everyone.

Question: How can confidence be developed in one who is humble, and humility in one who is confident?

First, see your life in the bigger context of time and space and then you will realize your life is nothing.

Second, those who are humble need to see that they are unique and dear to the Divine. This will bring confidence, and when you realize you are insignificant, that also brings confidence.

And third, having a guru will give you confidence and will culture humility in you. When you have a guru, you cannot be arrogant. The weakness in humility and the arrogance in confidence are removed, and you are left with confidence and humility.

Rishikesh, India
November 29, 2001

Humor is the buffer that saves you from humiliation. If you have a good sense of humor, you can never be humiliated, and if you refuse to be humiliated, you become invincible. Humor brings people together while humiliation tears them apart. In a society torn with humiliation and insults, humor is a breath of fresh air. A good sense of humor relieves you from fear and anxiety.

Humor should be coupled with care and concern. Mere humor, without care and concern or appropriate action, can irritate those who come to you with serious problems.

Humor can keep spirits high, yet if overdone it leaves a bad taste. Humor with wisdom creates an atmosphere of celebration, but humor without wisdom is shallow. Humor without sensitivity is satire and it comes back to you with more problems. The wise use humor to bring wisdom and to lighten every situation.

The intelligent use humor as a shield against humiliation. The cruel use humor as a sword to insult others. The irresponsible use humor to escape from responsibility. The fool takes humor too seriously! Humor is spontaneous; to make an effort to be humorous makes no sense.

Question: How does one cultivate a sense of humor?

Humor is not just words; it is the lightness of your Being. You can cultivate your sense of humor in many ways.

- Being cordial and lighthearted brings out authentic humor, while reading and repeating jokes will not.
- Do not take life too seriously, because you will never come out of it alive!
- Have a sense of belongingness with everybody, including those who are not friendly.
- Practice yoga and meditation.

- Have unshakable faith in the Divine and in the laws of karma.
- Be in the company of those who live in knowledge and who are humorous.
- Be willing to be a clown.

Bangalore Ashram, India
February 15, 2002

How would you like to see yourself – happy and bubbling with enthusiasm or dull and difficult to please?

Sometimes you like to be pleased, appeased and cajoled, so you put on a tough, troubled face and act difficult to please. It is so tiring for a person to appease and please ten people all the time. People who keep long faces and expect others to cajole and appease them, drive others away. Lovers often do this. They expend a lot of energy cajoling, reducing the joy and celebration of the moment.

It is all right to occasionally show how upset you are, but doing it repeatedly is taxing for you and the people you love.

If you feel down, appease and please yourself – do not expect others to do it. Your need to be appeased by someone else is a sign of grossness. This is the root of ignorance. If you want attention, all you get is tension.

It is not possible to attain divine love with a complaining face. The complaining face is a sign of an unaware mind. If you want to complain – complain to God or your guru because both have their ears covered!

Become one whose enthusiasm never dies, come what may.

Bangalore Ashram, India
September 21, 2000

Whatever you revere becomes bigger than you.

When you have reverence in all your relationships, then your own consciousness expands. Then to you even small things become big and significant. Every little creature becomes dignified. It is the reverence in a relationship that will save it.

When you have reverence for the whole universe, you are in harmony with the whole universe. And then you do not need to reject or renounce anything.

You often do not have reverence for what you own, and losing that reverence happens unconsciously. Reverence in ownership frees you from greed, jealousy and lust. Cultivate the skill of having reverence every moment of your life.

Bangalore Ashram, India
September 24, 2001

Adulation demonstrates the magnanimity of the one who adores, rather than the one who is adored. Adulation is a sign that the ego has become transparent; the best antidote for ego is adulation.

Adulation works in three ways. For an egoistic person, adulation for someone else is not palatable. If the adulation is for you, it boosts your ego. But if you adore someone else, it dissolves your ego and makes you magnanimous.

Desiring adulation is a sign of immaturity. Aversion to adulation is small-mindedness. A lack of adulation in life is dryness and boredom.

A healthy mind always likes to adore others, elevate them. An unhealthy mind likes to pull everything down.

Adulation indicates the trust, enthusiasm and richness of a culture. Lack of adulation indicates a society that is self-centered, small-minded, fearful and culturally impoverished.

Adulation does not sway the one who is great. The test of a person's greatness is that he is not shaken by any amount of adulation. Being indifferent to adulation when it comes to you and being magnanimous in giving it is the way of the wise.

Bangalore Ashram, India
November 15, 2001

For a flame to rise up, you need space above it. In the same way, for a man to rise up in his life, he needs an ideal, something to adore and worship. In worship, love, honor, respect and a sense of belongingness all come together. However, without a sense of belongingness, worship or idealism can lead to low self-esteem. Ancient people knew this so they insisted that people should feel a part of what they worship. They encouraged people to worship the sun, moon, mountains, rivers, plants, animals and other people.

Worship is the culmination of love and appreciation. Worship prevents love from turning into hatred or jealousy, and prevents appreciation from becoming low self-esteem. In life, if you do not adore or appreciate anything, you will be filled with negativity; a person who has nothing to worship or adore is sure to fall into depression.

Lack of adoration has led to many emotional, psychological and social problems in society. If you have nothing to hold high in life, selfishness, arrogance and violence are sure to follow. Adoring and honoring each other in society eliminates stress and fosters compassion and love.

In the previous century, it was thought that worshipping was an uncivilized and unintelligent thing to do. Worship was thought to rise from a slavish mentality. In fact it is just the contrary. Worship can only happen through gratefulness and not through subservience.

Worship in a true sense is a sign of maturity and not of weakness.

Question: You said worship is the culmination of love. Does worship also have a culmination?

The culmination of worship is self-knowledge, samadhi.

European Ashram, Bad Antogast, Germany
January 18, 2001

Divinity is unmanifest, but man has an innate desire to perceive the Divine in the manifest creation around him. He creates idols, breathes faith into them and requests Divinity to be present in the idols for awhile so that he can worship, express his love and play with the Divine. At the end of his worship he requests Divinity to go back into his heart from where it manifested. This is in all puja practices.

People do not actually worship the idols but instead worship the unmanifest Divinity which has all the Divine qualities. So, the idol worshippers of the East are not the same as those described in the Bible, because they are not just worshipping different gods and different idols, they are worshipping the one Divinity in many different forms.

Paganism, Satanism and animal worship, without the knowledge of the one Divinity, is very different from seeing the Divine in every form of the manifest universe. In the Eastern tradition, gods and goddesses are part of the one Divinity like the different colors of white sunlight, while in the Greek tradition, gods and goddesses are in themselves different and unique entities.

Worshipping Satan and different entities is completely unlike worshipping Divinity in its various forms. Every form belongs to the Divine. When you adore the form, you adore the Divinity behind the form.

With this knowledge, the very act of worship, which is more an inner phenomenon, assumes a more colorful and vibrant expression indicating that both the form and the formless are all Divine.

Rishikesh, India
March 22, 2001

Praising the fool benefits society!

A fool who is pleased might stop doing harm and start doing useful work. In this sense it is wise to praise a fool; it helps to motivate him. So your praise is meaningful when it is directed towards a fool.

A wise man by his nature will continue doing good work because his attitude does not depend on someone's praise or blame. So it serves no purpose to praise a wise man because your praise will have no impact on him.

There are three types of people – the wise, the crooked and the immature. The wise man continues doing good work whether he is scolded or praised. Crooked people need to be praised to get them to do good work. And from time to time immature people need to be both praised and scolded for them to do something good.

Rishikesh, India
March 22, 2002

When you are on a spiritual path, you are not thankful or obliged to anyone. In the Bhagavad Gita, Krishna says, "Na abhinandati na dveshthi" – he is dear to Me who neither goes on thanking people nor hates anyone.

Thanking and feeling obliged indicate that you believe in someone else's existence rather than in the Divine who rules everything. When you feel obliged, then you are not honoring the principles of karma or the Divine plan.

Appreciate people for what they are; do not thank them for what they do. Otherwise your thankfulness is centered around ego. Be grateful, but do not be grateful for an act. Be grateful for what is.

As every individual is nothing but a puppet of the one, thanking and feeling obliged simply demonstrates ignorance. Everything is ruled, controlled and managed by one Divinity. That consciousness has to shine forth in every act of yours; you do not need to make a mood of it.

Question: Guruji, we are so grateful to you so what should we do?

When you have a total sense of belonging, then gratitude does not become an obligation. Such gratitude is for the Divine only and this gratitude enhances your strength.

Agra, India
September16, 2000

Authenticity and skillfulness appear to be contradictory but in fact they are complementary. Your intentions need to be authentic and your actions need to be skillful. The more authentic the intention, the more skillful the action will be. Authentic intention and skillful action make you unshakable.

Skill is required only when authenticity cannot have its way. Yet skill without authenticity makes you shallow. You cannot have an authentic action and a skillful intention. If you try to be authentic in your action but manipulative in your mind, then that is when mistakes happen.

Question: Is it possible to have a powerful intention, like greed, that is authentic?

If your intention is colored by such emotions as greed or over-ambition, then your intention is not authentic. Whenever your intentions are impure, it pricks your consciousness, so it cannot be authentic. Authentic intentions are free from negative emotions. An action that is not skillful leads to negative emotions and an intention that is not authentic harbors negative emotions.

Question: How do we best deal with intentions?

Do not keep any sankalpas, or intentions, to yourself. Offer them to the Divine.

Actions can never be perfect but our intentions can be perfect. Actions always have room for improvement. Action implies growth and movement, and that needs space.

The depth in you and the freedom in you bring out all the skillfulness in you. Krishna was the most skillful because his silence was so deep.

Washington, D.C., United States
June 27, 2001

Action comes out of conscious decision. Reaction comes out of impulsiveness. Impulsiveness creates a chain of karma.

Reaction and non-action both create karma, but conscious action transcends karma. Although conscious action does not create new karma, non-action can. A soldier shooting in war and a policeman using tear gas do not create karma, but a doctor who fails to give medicine to a patient in need incurs karma.

Through knowledge and devotion, transcend all karma and be free.

European Ashram, Bad Antogast, Germany
July 27, 2000

Love and authority are totally opposite values, yet they co-exist.

The grosser the consciousness, the more pronounced must be authority. The more refined and subtle the consciousness, the less need to exercise authority.

When you are unrefined, you demand authority and when you demand authority, love recedes. Asserting authority indicates a lack of confidence and love. The more evident one's authority, the less sensitive and effective it will be.

A sensible person will not demand authority at all but will assume it. The most effective business leaders will not impose their authority, will not make you feel it, for authority can never bring inspiration.

Your sincere servant has more authority over you than your boss. A baby has full authority over his mother. Similarly, a devotee has complete authority over the Divine, though he never exercises it.

- The less love you have, the more pronounced will be your authority.
- The greater your love, the subtler will be your authority.
- The subtler you become, the more authority you gain.

Bangalore Ashram, India
August 16, 2001

Usually where there is aishwarya – lordship – there is no madhurya – sweetness – and where there is madhurya, there is no aishwarya. Where life has blossomed fully, there is both.

Aishwarya means ishwaratva – lordship of that which "Is." Wealth is also referred to as aishwarya, because wealth commands a certain amount of authority.

Can love and authority co-exist? Only in a fully blossomed Being is there both lordship and sweetness. There was aishwarya in Sri Rama, but only glimpses of madhurya. In Parshuram's life there was only lordship, but no madhurya. Buddha manifested more madhurya – the sweetness – and less authority. But Krishna manifested both and so did Jesus. There was lordship when they said, "I am the way," and there was sweetness in their expressions of prayer and love.

Bangalore Ashram, India
October 31, 2001

In a congregation, Sri Sri asked, "How many of you feel strong?" Many people raised their hands.

Sri Sri then asked, "Why?"

"Because you are with us," they answered.

"Only those who feel weak can surrender," Sri Sri responded.

All those who were feeling strong were taken aback; suddenly they felt weak!

If you are in love, you feel weak because love makes you weak. Yet there is no power stronger than love. Love is strength. Love is the greatest power on earth. You feel absolutely powerful when you are with the Divine.

Question: But why do we keep alternating between strength and weakness?

That is the fluctuation in life.

When you feel weak – surrender.
When you feel strong – do seva.

New Delhi, India
August 10, 2000

I am the valentine of the whole world and I reside in every heart. If you are my valentine, you will see me everywhere. Have the same love for everyone, but with different flavors. You cannot behave the same way with everyone, but you can love all of them the same. Love transcends behavior and etiquette.

London, United Kingdom
February 14, 1996

Just Be

Joy is dissolving...losing your identity.
Rest is dissolving...losing your identity.
Love is dissolving...losing your identity.
The message for this new year is...just be!
Relax and just be.
That does not mean be lazy...No!
Be very busy...and just be.

Events come and go, they perish like flowers. But every event and every person contains some honey. Like a bee, just take the honey out of every event and every moment and move on. Be like a busy bee and be in the Being.

Question: What is the nectar of life?

The Infinity...the Divinity.

How do you like it?

Weggis, Switzerland
January 5, 1996

In a state of ignorance, imperfection is natural and perfection is an effort.

In a state of wisdom or enlightenment, imperfection is an effort but perfection is a compulsion and is unavoidable.

Perfection means taking total responsibility, and total responsibility means knowing that you are the only responsible person in the whole world. When you think that others are responsible, then your degree of responsibility diminishes.

When you are in total vairagya – dispassion – you take care of even trivial and insignificant things with such perfection. For example, during every morning puja, Sri Sri decorates the puja table with such great care, choosing flowers in different color combinations and patterns every day, fully knowing that the decoration will not last even ten minutes. After the puja he then removes the garlands and showers people with the flowers. Yet even while he is in a deep state of samadhi, he effortlessly and lovingly decorates the puja table everyday. It is obvious that it does not matter how the flowers are arranged – attention to such a trivial thing with such keen awareness can only come through utter dispassion.

Perfection is the very nature of the enlightened one.

Bangalore Ashram, India
October 12, 2000

There are three types of dispassion.

The first type is the dispassion that arises when you realize the misery in the world and you fear misery. The events in life – the pain and suffering you experience or see – bring dispassion.

The second type of dispassion is born out of your desire to achieve something higher. Some consider dispassion as a path to enlightenment – by renouncing something here they hope to gain something out there. They engage in austerities and take vows to have a better place in heaven.

The third type of dispassion comes from wisdom or knowledge. A broader understanding of the transient nature of things cultures a state of non-attachment to events, objects, people, or situations, and this lets you remain calm and unperturbed.

Divine love does not let dispassion manifest. The attainment of love brings such bliss and such intoxication that it not only takes away your passion, but dispassion as well.

Jakarta, Java, Indonesia
May 26, 2002

Sanyas means what? "I am nothing and I want nothing," or "I am everything and I have everything." It is being either colorless or multicolored.

Bangalore Ashram, India

May 2, 1996

Passion makes you weak. Dispassion is strength.

For your passion to be fulfilled, you must depend upon so many things. Passion and self-reliance do not go together. If you are passionate, you need to forget about being self-reliant. If you want to be self-reliant, you must drop your passion.

Your spirit is what brings together these two completely different aspects in you. The same spirit that wants self-reliance is also passionate. It is only in spirituality that passion and dispassion can happen together. This combination is the rarest.

When you are dispassionate, you have strength, and strength is self-reliance. True self-reliance is realizing that nothing is excluded from the Self. And when you realize everything is part of the Self, then you can be passionate about everything. To fulfill your passion, you need to rely only on the Self, for Self alone is non-changing.

In truth, there is neither reliance nor passion. Usually, you are either passionate or self-reliant. But in an elevated state of consciousness, you can be neither, or both.

Bangalore Ashram, India
February 22, 2001

Often when you are happy you feel life is a dream because you do not believe it is real. When there is misery you feel life is a burden, and sometimes your misery is because you take trivial things too seriously. But if you have really gone through pleasure, you realize that pleasure is a burden, and if you have thoroughly undergone misery, you realize that life is a dream. When you realize that you have been carried through every miserable situation, then you know life is a dream. And in between the pleasure and the pain, life is all a joke.

Life is very uncertain. Before it takes you away, realize it is a dream, a burden or a joke.

Question: What about life is a joke?

You do not question a joke. If you question a joke, it is no longer a joke. Do not question a burden either. It is a waste of time to question life and its events.

A burden makes you go deep. It takes you to the core of yourself. Awareness of dreaming wakes you up and seeing life as a joke makes you light.

The only certainty is that life is a dream, a burden or a joke, and only when you realize this can you be centered.

Montreal Ashram, Canada
May 10, 2001

It is often believed that glory and dispassion are contradictory and cannot co-exist. Glory and luxury without dispassion is a nauseating pomp and show. Such glory does not bring fulfillment for anyone; it is shallow. Alternatively, the dispassion that is afraid of glory is weak. True dispassion is oblivious to glory.

The glory that comes with dispassion is something that is true; it is permanent and authentic. When someone chases after glory, they are shallow. Movie stars, politicians and religious leaders who try to hold on to their status, to their glory, are certain to lose it. If you run after glory, all that you get is misery. When you are dispassionate, glory comes to you.

If you are afraid of glory, that means you are not well-grounded in dispassion. In India the sadhus run away from glory. They think they will lose their dispassion and get trapped in the web of the world, in the circus. The dispassion is so blissful that they get attached to it. They are afraid of losing the dispassion, the centeredness and the bliss that comes with it. This is weak dispassion.

Dispassion is a state of Being and glory is the happening around it. True dispassion can never be lost or overshadowed by glory. True dispassion is glorious. Real glory is true dispassion.

Cascade, Colorado, United States
January 16, 2002

Do not use dispassion to push away the fire of longing for the Divine or for satsang. There is a little fire in you that propels you toward knowledge, sadhana, devotion and service but sometimes you use knowledge to put out that fire. So-called dispassionate people are often morose and unenthusiastic. Often you will hear people say, "Oh, never mind, God is everywhere, Guruji is in my heart, I can do satsang anywhere.

My seva is my sadhana, so there is no need to meditate. Anyway I am doing sadhana twenty-four hours a day. When God wills, He will call me to satsang and Advanced Courses again." Such excuses should not be justified as dispassion.

When you want to do some service, the mind says, "Oh, it is all maya anyway; everything is an illusion. It is all just happening. Things will happen when the time comes."

In this way knowledge gets misused and is quoted out of context to suit one's convenience or laziness. When you use knowledge like this you miss a lot. This is when dispassion is detrimental.

In the name of dispassion do not lose that spark of enthusiasm and interest. Keep alive the fire of longing for the Divine and for service to society.

Montreal Ashram, Canada
January 24, 2002

What is enthusiasm? Enthusiasm means to be connected to God within. When you are with your source, you can only be enthusiastic and you cannot be anything but enthusiastic when your mind is totally in the present moment. Apathy is when you are away from the source of life.

You should know that dispassion is not apathy; it is simply a broader perspective of reality. Dispassion is moving towards the source. Dispassion simply means the way back home. It is the journey towards the source, which is a reservoir of enthusiasm.

When dispassion and enthusiasm co-exist, that is the secret of perennial enthusiasm and profound dispassion. Though they appear to be opposite, they are actually complementary.

Washington, D.C., United States
July 1, 2002

Reason is constrained in the known. Faith is moving in the unknown.
Reason is repetition. Faith is exploration.
Reason is routine. Faith is adventure.
Reason and faith are completely opposite, yet they are both integral parts of life.

Not having faith is itself misery; faith gives instant comfort. While reason keeps you sane and grounded, no miracle can happen without faith. Faith takes you beyond limitations. In faith you can transcend the laws of nature, but it needs to be pure. Faith is beyond reason, yet you need to have faith in your own reasoning! Faith and reason cannot exist without each other. Every reason is based on some faith. Whenever reason or faith break down, confusion and chaos prevail – and this is often a step towards growth.

There are two types of faith. Faith that is born out of fear, greed and insecurity, or faith born out of love like the faith between the mother and child or the master and disciple. While the faith that is born of love cannot be broken, the faith that comes out of fear and greed is shaky.

An atheist bases himself on reason, and a believer bases himself on faith. An atheist rationalizes to keep his eyes shut to reality. A believer uses God as an insurance policy – he thinks he is special. But in the eyes of God there is no "mine" and "others" – all are the same. Death shakes them both! When someone close dies, the eyes of an atheist are opened, and a believer's faith cracks. Only a Yogi – a wise one – remains unshaken, for that person has transcended both reason and faith.

You need to balance faith and reason.

European Ashram, Bad Antogast, Germany
May 16, 2001

Question: Guruji, how can we control daydreams?

What is daydreaming? Daydreaming is simply when you have a desire but you do not have the faith that you can achieve it. You can control daydreaming by having a strong goal and believing in it. Like the scientist who wanted to go to the moon and kept dreaming about it – for him it was the goal of his life but for others it was just a daydream.

You either drop the idea that your dream will happen or you believe it will.

When you do not know yourself – your true potential – you have no faith or confidence in your dreams.

Once you have faith and confidence in your dreams, they are no longer daydreams.

New Delhi, India
December 7, 2001

Faith and alertness appear to be completely opposite in nature. When you are alert, there is usually no faith and you feel restless and insecure. When you have faith, your mind in a restful state and you feel secure, so you are not alert.

There are three types of faith.

Tamasic faith is caused by dullness. For example, when you do not want to take responsibility or action and you say, "Oh, it doesn't matter, God will take care of all these things!"

Rajasic faith is brought on by an intense compulsion of desires and ambition. The ambition keeps your faith alive.

Satvic faith is innocent and is born out of fullness of consciousness.

Faith and alertness, though apparently opposite in nature, are actually complementary to each other. In the absence of faith there can be no growth and without alertness there can be no correct understanding. Faith can make you complacent while alertness makes you tense. If there is no faith, there is fear. And when there is no alertness, you cannot perceive or express properly, so a combination of both is essential.

In Gyana – state of wisdom – there is alertness without tension and faith without complacency. The purpose of education should be to remove the element of dullness from faith and the element of fear from alertness. This is a unique and rare combination. If you have faith and alertness at the same time, then you will become a true Gyani – a wise one.

Bangalore Ashram, India
June 17, 2002

Why would someone tell a lie to their dear ones or to their beloved?

This is a question often asked by lovers. Love cannot stand untruth; it causes relationships to fall apart. The answer lies in understanding the paradox of love and truth.

People tell lies just to save and maintain their love. Lies are a result of fear that the truth might damage the love between husband and wife, boyfriend and girlfriend, parents and children.

In love you feel weak but truth brings strength. So why do people prefer love over truth, weakness over strength?

No one wants to sacrifice love. Thus people are ready to give up the truth for their love. Love takes the luster out of truth. Sometimes truth can make love bitter; while in love, even lies can appear sweet, like Krishna's lies to his mother, Yashoda.

The truth that does not nourish love makes no sense and the love that cannot withstand the truth is not true love. When you are assured that your love is so strong that the truth can neither break it nor cause bitterness, then the truth prevails and love shines.

With truth there are judgments, but true love is beyond judgments. Thus true love makes you weak and yet it is the greatest strength.

Bangalore Ashram, India
February 22, 2002

CHAPTER TWO

The Path to the Goal That is You

Become God to each other. Do not look for God somewhere in the sky, but see God in every pair of eyes, in the mountains, in water, in trees and in animals. How? Only when you see God in yourself will this happen. Only God can worship God. To recognize Divinity, there are three dimensions – time, space and mind.

For seekers, it is necessary to honor time and space so they can experience sacredness in their minds. When you honor time and space, your mind becomes alert. But for the one who has transcended the mind, either sacredness has no meaning or all times, every place and every mood is sacred.

Precious moments are few in life. Catch them and treasure them. Place, time and the mood of your mind are factors that influence celebration. Snatch every opportunity to celebrate. Then you will feel great and full. Then celebration infiltrates your mind in all moods and space, and celebration is inevitable. Celebration reminds you of the fullness of the moment. The moments you are in the company of knowledge – the master – are the most precious moments in your life. Treasure them. Treasuring them, you transcend the mind, time and space. That is true celebration.

Lake Tahoe, California, United States
July 8, 2001

Navratri means the nine nights and the new night. Creation happens in darkness – in the womb of the mother and underneath the soil. Nine months in the womb are like nine long nights where the spirit takes human form. These nine nights are precious, as they enrich the subtle energy of creation. Night also provides rest and rejuvenation. At night all of creation goes to sleep. Working people come home at night and celebrate, rejoice and pray.

There are 64 Divine Mother impulses which govern the subtle aspects of creation. These impulses are responsible for restoring all earthly and spiritual benefits, and are part of one's awakened consciousness. These nine nights are celebrated to rekindle those divine impulses and to celebrate the innermost depth of our lives.

Minsk, Russia
October 9, 1996

When you love something, you have a sense of belongingness with it. You can only love something when it belongs to you. If it is not yours, you cannot love it. Love is the shadow of the Self.

The bigger the Self, the bigger the shadow and the bigger the love.

When love is cast over all of creation, then you are the Big Self. That is Lordship.

When Lordship dawns in the Self, there is perennial celebration.

Bangalore Ashram, India
October 26, 2000

One who is not amazed by the magnificence of this creation – his eyes are not yet opened. Once your eyes are open, they close, and this is called meditation.

Tell me, what in this creation is not a mystery? Birth is a mystery; death is a mystery. If both birth and death are mysteries, then life is certainly a greater mystery, isn't it?

Being completely immersed in the mystery of life and in this creation is samadhi.

Your knowing or believing does not really matter to what Is. This creation is an unfathomable secret and its mysteries only deepen.

Getting steeped in mystery is devotion. The "scene" is a mystery; the "seer" is a mystery. Deepening the mystery of creation is science. Deepening the mystery of the Self is spirituality. They are the two sides of the same coin.

If neither science nor spirituality can create wonder and devotion in you, then you are in deep slumber.

Bangalore Ashram, India
October 7, 2000

After a satsang, a group met with Sri Sri and were playing with words, arguing with him and teasing him by telling him that he does not spend much time with them and yet has stolen their hearts. Sri Sri kept winning by twisting their arguments. He went on to say:

Whether you win or lose an argument with me, you still laugh. Normally what happens to you when you lose an argument? You are sad and upset, hurt and angry. But when you lose or win an argument with me, you are still happy. Why? Because you have a total sense of belongingness; your love is more important than perfection, comfort and desires; you are able to put your Being before a happening; and you have confidence in the ultimate good. When there is a total sense of belongingness, real play happens. Winning or losing is irrelevant.

Can you have this same attitude with everyone?

Bangalore Ashram, India
September 5, 1996

You are the Christmas tree. The Christmas tree is pointing upwards and its branches grow on all sides. It is orderly. At the time of year when no tree bears anything, it has many gifts to offer. And it is green throughout the year. A Christmas tree bears the gifts and the lights not for itself. All the gifts you are carrying in your life are for others. Anyone who comes to you, you offer them your gifts.

European Ashram, Bad Antogast, Germany
December 24, 1997

Suppose the worst of the world is given to you; what would you do with it? You cannot complain if you get the worst. You can only complain if you do not get the worst. If the world is at its worst, then it can only get better and you are here to make it better.

What happens when you have to do it all by yourself, when no one helps? Your options are to be frustrated and complain; to take credit that you did it by yourself, and thank others for not helping so that you could take all the credit; and to be grateful, pray deeply, and know that you got all the energy needed to do it alone.

There is only one doer.

Dallas, Texas, United States
January 22, 1997

People who are willing to serve will have good times even in the bad times. When there are problems, such as famine or war, Red Cross people are fine as they are serving. The more relief they bring, the happier they feel. And people who are selfish and who just want to enjoy themselves will be miserable even in good times. Often the organizers of a party do not enjoy the party because some little thing is missing, they forgot to invite somebody, somebody did not come or some little thing went wrong.

A wise one is happy even in bad times. And the ignorant one is unhappy even in good times. You make the time good or bad. People usually blame the bad time and just wait for the good time. Even if an astrologer says that you are in a hopeless time, you can still make it a good time!

Like weather, time has its impact on you. Your satsangs and sadhana are your shield, your protection. So realize that you are more than time and that you can change the time by your connection to the Divine.

European Ashram, Bad Antogast, Germany
New Years Eve 1997

Always know that the Divine never gives you a responsibility you cannot fulfill. No one ever expects you to treat them if you are not a doctor. No one will ask you to fix their wiring system if you are not an electrician.

- Your responsibility is only what you can do.
- And you do not know what you can do.
- Always accept that you do not know what you can do.
- Ignorance of your capability can expand you.

When you know what you can do, you can progress. But when you do not know what you can do, you can grow by leaps and bounds.

When you know what you can do, you can do things. When you do not know what you can do, you can do things even better!

Bangalore Ashram, India
October 18, 2000

God created humanity and the whole world with so many different varieties, so many good things. God made so many types of vegetables and fragrances, flowers and thorns, dragons and horrors, to please humans and to keep them entertained. But humanity became more and more depressed.

Then God acted tough and humans had to start pleasing Him. So humans kept themselves busy pleasing God and they became happier since they had no time to get worried or depressed. When you have someone to please, it keeps you on your toes and you are happier. But if your goal is just to please yourself, depression is sure to follow.

Pleasure simply brings more craving but the problem is that we try to get contentment through pleasure. True contentment can only come through service.

European Ashram, Bad Antogast, Germany
August 2, 2001

Who is a volunteer? A volunteer is someone who comes to help without being asked. Someone who is self-motivated and inspired becomes a volunteer.

It is possible for a volunteer's inspirational motivation to diminish, which can bring frustration. Usually a volunteer's attitude comes from demand rather than humility, and this dilutes the quality of the service. Another downfall for volunteers is that they slip away from commitment, thinking there is no "boss," thinking, "If I like it, I'll do it; if I don't like it, I won't do it!" It is like the steering wheel of a car – if all the tires say they do not need to be steered, then the car cannot move forward. If you want to construct a building, you have to accept the authority of the structural engineer, the "boss."

All these problems can be overcome only by being more grounded in spiritual knowledge. A volunteer devoid of spirituality is utterly weak.

- A volunteer needs to remain faithful to his commitment.
- The integrity of a volunteer comes from his spiritual practices.
- A volunteer must accept the leader of the project.
- The strength of a volunteer is based on the challenges he is ready and willing to face.
- A volunteer moves beyond boundaries when he finds he is capable of doing so much more than he ever thought of doing.
- A true volunteer does not expect appreciation or reward and he who thinks he is obliging someone is thoroughly mistaken.

A person volunteers because he derives joy from it. That joy itself is the reward, and it is immediate. It does not come on the first of every month in the form of a salary. When a volunteer realizes this, he is filled with gratitude.

When a volunteer waivers from within, his support is knowledge and good friends.

Taipei, Taiwan
November 9, 2001

Many people do not want to work under someone else, be it in their profession, in a company, or even as a volunteer. The notion is that when you work under someone, you lose your freedom and you have to be accountable for your work.

Thus many people opt for their own business, wanting to be their own boss. But in your own business, you are accountable to so many people. If you cannot be accountable to even one person, how can you be accountable to many? This is the paradox. In fact, having your own business binds you more than having a boss!

Refusing to work under someone is a sign of weakness, not strength. A strong person feels comfortable working under anyone, because he knows his strength. It is the weak and poor in spirit who do not like to work under someone else because they are unaware of their strength. They cannot be successful in business or in any profession. Even working under a wise person, those who are timid and weak in spirit will be uncomfortable. But those who know their strength, effectively work even under a fool!

The same applies to volunteers. Often volunteers do not want to work under someone else, but this merely demonstrates their weakness. With such an attitude, they achieve very little.

Question: How do I deal with the frustration of working under a fool?

When you know your strength, with skill and intelligence you can turn every disadvantage into an advantage. A fool can bring out the best in your communication skills!

So watch out! If you feel uncomfortable working under someone, it clearly shows you need to strengthen yourself. Desiring freedom from circumstances, situations or people is not freedom at all. Knowing that nobody can take away your freedom – that is strength. And when you realize your strength is unshakable, you will be able to work under anyone.

Rishikesh, India
March 30, 2001

There are five types of seva.

The first type is the seva done when you do not even know that you are doing it. You do not recognize it as seva because it is your very nature – you cannot help doing it!

The second type is the seva that you do because it is needed for that situation.

The third type of seva is done because it gives you joy.

The fourth type is done out of your desire for merit – you do seva expecting some benefit in the future.

And the fifth type is when you do seva just to show off, to improve your image and to gain social or political recognition. Such seva is simply exhausting, while the first type does not bring any tiredness at all!

To improve the quality of your seva, regardless of where you start, you must move up to the higher levels.

Bangalore Ashram, India
November 23, 2001

Knowledge has organizing power. Only knowledge can organize. The more steeped you are in knowledge, the better you can organize. These seven principles will make you effective and will build a strong team.

◆ Never underestimate your organization. If you underestimate your organization, you will not be able to build it.

◆ Defend your intentions, not your actions. Often people defend their actions and lose sight of their intentions. Then they feel sorry and weak. There is no need to feel sorry. Defend your intention to do right.

◆ Teamwork. With teamwork you achieve more than you do individually. Some work is best done alone and other work is best done with a team. Find the balance between walking alone and working with a team. In either case, alone or with a team, you will face obstacles. For your growth, both are essential. Each has its disadvantages and advantages. Drop either one, and you will be at a loss. The skill is not to have an aversion to either and to focus on the goal.

◆ Defending friends. Suppose you have introduced a friend to a job and they make a mistake. Do not try to defend them. That is where the team breaks up. When you defend a friend, you are not friendly to everybody. Defending someone's mistakes does not do justice to the team and stops the person from learning. Soft-heartedness and compassion in an organization can be detrimental to both the teamwork and the organization.

◆ Never justify a mistake with intimidation or logic. Raising your voice, intimidation, anger, shouting, and applying erroneous logic make a wrong appear right. Someone may do something wrong, but with shouting he makes the wrong appear right. Raising your voice and asserting through intimidation may make a wrong appear right. Do not give in to that. Do not give into assertiveness, intimidation, wrong logic and soft-heartedness.

◆ Volunteers often act as though everyone is a boss and not a worker. When working with volunteers, be calm and quiet. Ask, "Have you finished your work?"

◆ Solutions will always be ad hoc. The more dynamic an institution is, the more the solutions will be ad hoc. It's not like a nine-to-five company job where roles are designed and planned for a year. With volunteers, the productivity is more intense. The more dynamic a group, the quicker things happen. Maintaining a margin for confusion and chaos can prevent stress.

Bangalore Ashram, India
December 16, 1999

So many people are stuck with what is "important." They are always caught up in thinking about what is important. Why must you only do what is important? When you say something is important, you are limiting your vastness.

For something to be important, many things must be unimportant, so you cannot eliminate unimportant things. It is important to have unimportant things to make something else important. Things are either themselves important or they make other things important. So that means everything is important, and…everything is unimportant. When you realize this fact, you have no more choices to make.

A journalist once asked me, "Why is it important to breathe?" "Why is it important to be happy?" "Why is it important to have peace?" These questions are not relevant at all. Why should you always look for what is important? Something that is unimportant can contribute to something that is important. And what is important and unimportant changes with time and space. Food is important when you are hungry and unimportant when you are full.

When something is inevitable, you do not categorize it as important or unimportant. It is beyond choice.

"Everything is important" is karma yoga. "Nothing is important" is deep meditation.

Montreal Ashram, Canada
January 11, 2001

Secretaries, police, judges, accountants and people in key positions should not be friendly!

The disadvantages of being friendly are:

- You come under obligation.
- You lose your freedom.
- You become prone to picking up bad habits and negative moods.
- Your perception cannot be free and fair. Your thoughts and actions may not be impartial.
- Your focus, commitment, creativity and above all, your time will be wasted.

It takes much wisdom to be free from the burden of obligation and not be influenced by your friends' opinions and feelings.

On many occasions, it is better to be unfriendly than friendly. Being unfriendly does not mean being aggressive and inimical. The best secretaries, personal assistants, security personnel and judges have to be unfriendly.

Those who are aloof and indifferent get centered more quickly than those who are too friendly. A certain degree of aloofness in every relationship will strengthen your personality and connect you to your source.

It is easy to be aloof or unfriendly. But to be friendly and aloof is sadhana.

En route from Davos to Zurich Airport, Switzerland
January 31, 2001

There is pleasure in rest and pleasure in activity. The pleasure in activity is momentary and causes fatigue while the pleasure in rest is magnanimous and energizing. So to the one who has tasted pleasure in rest (samadhi), the pleasure in activity is insignificant. All activities that you do, you do so that you can have deep rest. Activity is part of the system. However, the real pleasure is in samadhi. In order to have deep rest one must be active. The proper balance of both is essential.

Many seek pleasure in this or that, but the wise man just smiles. The real rest is only in knowledge.

Montreal Ashram, Quebec, Canada
July 19, 2001

What can you do for eternity? You definitely cannot do anything that is big or great because that requires effort and effort tires you. So, doing something great is a temporary state. If you can think of one thing that is far beneath your capacity and agree to do it for eternity, that becomes puja.

The willingness to consciously do trivial things for eternity unites you with eternity. This is an antidote to ego. Ego is always ambitious and strives to do the toughest job, like climbing Mount Everest. Simple acts like watching a butterfly, watering the garden, observing the sky can bring deep relaxation, and relaxation connects you with your source. This does not mean that you should do trivial things all your life, but consciously agreeing to do trivial acts for eternity opens a new dimension and brings immense peace and restfulness.

To find rest in activity, choose an activity that is far below your capacity and agree to do it for eternity. Doing a job far below your capacity and being satisfied will then make it possible to do a job much beyond your capacity.

Know that all actions are born out of infinity and that which is born out of infinity can take you to infinity.

Kodaikanal, India
May 24, 2001

What should you do if your commitment is boring?

Commitment has value when things are not so charming. When things are interesting you do not need commitment at all. You never say you are committed to doing something that is very interesting or charming.

Washington, D.C., United States
July 2, 2002

Question: Why is it easier for some of us to commit to our own welfare rather than to the welfare of others?

Because you do not know that whatever you are committed to brings you strength. If you are committed to your family, then your family supports you. If you are committed to your society, you enjoy the support of society. If you are committed to God, God gives you strength. If you are committed to truth, truth brings you strength.

Often people are not aware of this and that is why they are hesitant to commit to a greater cause. They also fear that commitment weakens people or takes away their freedom. But your commitment to a cause is bound to bring you comfort in the long run.

Commitment in life will certainly move you toward a higher cause. The higher the commitment, the greater is the good for all.

When your path is charming, commitment is effortless and is part of your nature.

Boston, Massachusetts, United States
April 27, 2002

A commitment can only be felt when it oversteps convenience. When something is convenient, it is not called commitment. If you are driven by your convenience, your commitment falls apart causing more inconvenience! If you keep dropping your commitment because it is inconvenient, can you be comfortable? Often what is convenient does not bring comfort but just gives an illusion of comfort. Also if you are too stuck in commitment, and it is inconvenient too often, you will be unable to fulfill your commitment and it will only generate frustration. Wisdom is to strike a balance between convenience and commitment because both bring comfort to the body, mind and spirit.

A seeker of knowledge should forget about convenience, as should soldiers, rulers, students, seekers of wealth and all essential service providers. Those who want to be creative and adventurous need to transcend convenience. Those who are ambitious and have a passion for a goal will not care for convenience. Commitment is comfort to the wise. Whenever their commitment is shaken, their comfort is also shaken. To the lazy, commitment is torture though it is their best remedy. In the long run, commitment will always bring comfort.

Question: Are there any commitments that can be given up?

Yes. Sometimes when you make a commitment without a vision, you feel stifled when your vision expands. Such commitments made with shortsightedness can be given up.

- A smaller, less important commitment can be given up for a greater commitment.
- Commitment to the means can be given up for the sake of a commitment to the goals.
- When in the long run, your commitment brings misery to many it can be given up.

Bali, Indonesia
April 5, 2001

All the scriptures of the world glorify sacrifice. But what is sacrifice?

It is giving up something you value. You can only sacrifice something that you would like to keep for yourself, something that gives you pleasure and joy. You cannot sacrifice something that you dislike or disown.

Sacrifice is always related to a higher cause for a greater good. At the same time, when your love for the greater good is so strong, nothing else assumes any value. Sacrifice here becomes irrelevant, because love alone is your strongest driving force. When there is so much love, there cannot be sacrifice and when there is no love, there is no sacrifice.

If a mother has made plans to see a movie and she realizes that her child is sick, she does not say that she sacrificed the movie to care for her child because she simply did not want to go. Nothing else charms the mother besides being with her child.

You do not sacrifice something for someone you love. Sacrifice indicates that your pleasure has more value than the cause for which you are sacrificing. When love is lukewarm, then sacrifice assumes meaning. Yet sacrifice purifies the human mind and reins in selfish tendencies. It can also bring pride, arrogance, self-pity and sometimes even depression.

You can sacrifice only that which you value. For a wise man nothing is more valuable than truth, values and the Divine, and he will never sacrifice those. God is the greatest, and if someone values the greatest, how can he sacrifice God? This is the paradox of sacrifice.

Rishikesh, India
March 15, 2001

When a river meets the ocean, the river no longer remains a river. It becomes the ocean. A drop of the ocean is part of the ocean. In the same way, the moment a devotee meets or surrenders to the Divine, the devotee becomes God. When the river meets the ocean, it recognizes that it is the ocean from the beginning to the end. Similarly, the individual "I... I..." dissolves into one Divinity.

Question: What about backwaters?

Sometimes the ocean goes into the river to greet it. Sometimes it seems that the ocean is pushing back the river. Similarly, the Divine puts questions and doubts in the mind or provides an amazing experience to bring you back home.

Bangalore Ashram, India
September 28, 2000

Do you know why the earth is shaped like a globe?

So you can kick it and it will roll away! From the moment you wake up in the morning you are always with people and your mind is caught up in worldly thoughts. So sometime during the day, sit for a few minutes, get into the cave of your heart, close your eyes, and kick the world away like a ball.

But as soon as you open your eyes, hold onto the ball because you need to kick it again in the next session. During the day be one hundred percent attached to your work; do not try to detach yourself. But when you sit for meditation, then totally detach yourself. Only those who can totally detach can take total responsibility.

Eventually you will be able to be both attached and detached simultaneously. Kick the ball and be in the goal. This is the art of living, the skill of living.

Montreal Ashram, Canada
January 4, 2001

Do not make an effort to impress others or to express yourself. Your effort to impress someone will be futile. Your effort to express yourself becomes an impediment. If you do not try to impress, expression comes naturally. When you come from the Self, your expression will be perfect and your impression lasts for ages.

Often you do not seem to have a control over your impressions and expressions. Wisdom is selecting your impressions and expressions. Enlightenment is when you do not have any impressions at all, whether good or bad. Then you "master" the art of expression. Many impressions in the mind cause confusion, distraction, chaos, an inability to focus, and ultimately, derangement of the mind. Nature has built into us a system through which we release some of the impressions – through dreams and meditation.

You lose depth, luster, and your serenity with excessive expression. Meditation erases the impressions and improves the expression.

Calcutta, India
April 2, 1998

Cleanse your body and cleanse your soul. Cleanse your body with water, your soul with knowledge and your spirit with pranayama and Kriya. There is no penance higher than pranayama. It is the greatest penance.

Minsk, Russia
October 9, 1996

A strong tendency to keep doing something, whether important or unimportant, becomes an impediment to meditation. "Doing" starts first with an intention and then translates into action. Though intention springs from Being, when it becomes "doing" it does not let you settle down. All intentions, good or bad, important or trivial, need to be dropped for meditation to happen.

Question: But isn't dropping all intentions itself an intention?

Yes, but that intention is necessary and it is the last. Dropping intentions is not an act. Just the intention to drop them itself serves the purpose. Dropping all intentions even for a moment brings you in touch with your Self and in that instant meditation happens.

While you sit for meditation, you have to let the world be the way it is. The repetition of meditation is to habituate your system to stop and start activity at will. The ability to consciously do this is a very precious skill.

Bangalore Ashram, India
October 29, 2001

Peace is your nature, yet you remain restless.

- Freedom is your nature, yet you remain in bondage.
- Happiness is your nature, yet you become miserable for some reason or another.
- Contentment is your nature, yet you continue to reel in desires.
- Benevolence is your nature, yet you do not reach out.
- Moving towards your nature is sadhana.
- Sadhana is becoming what you truly are!
- Your true nature is Shiva.
- And Shiva is peace, infinity, beauty and the non-dual One.

Ratri means "to take refuge." Shivaratri is taking refuge in Shiva.

Rishikesh, India
March 16, 2002

Rest and happiness make a real holiday. Often people go on a holiday and they come back tired and tanned, needing a few more days to recuperate! A real holiday is one that energizes you and does not wear you out. Nothing energizes you like wisdom, so remember:

- Doubts and complaints are impediments to rest.
- The moment you set out on your holiday, know that it has begun. Often people expect to find a pinnacle of happiness. Enjoy every moment of the journey as children do; do not wait for the destination.
- If you cannot be happy in one place, you cannot be happy in any other place. If you do not know how to row one boat, you will not be able to row any other boat.
- To get maximum satisfaction out of your holiday, you need to do something creative and to engage in seva.
- Do not ever forget to make meditation and prayer a part of your holiday.

If your days are holy, then every day is a holiday.

New Delhi, India
March 31, 2002

Are you special or ordinary? By being on the path what makes you special? Your perception, observation and expression have advanced. That which makes you ordinary by being on the path is that you are special. Everybody thinks they are very special in some way.

Your perception has improved. You see the cause behind every cause – the Divine, and you see the great plan behind every small plan. You do not see intentions behind other's mistakes and you are not a doubting Thomas – the apostle who doubted Jesus.

Your observation has improved. Before getting onto the path you never observed your emotions. Now you observe your emotions, positive or negative, love or hate, anger or compassion, pain or pleasure.

Your expression has improved. In the central core of everyone there are all good qualities. In those who are unfortunate and stressed, they have not expressed these great qualities, but you have given an expression to them.

Grimstad, Norway
August 28, 1996

Often you are in a rush in life. When you are in a rush, you are unable to perceive things properly. This takes the charm, thrill and beauty from your life. You can never be close to the truth when you are in a rush because your perception, observation and expression become distorted.

The rush to enjoy robs the joy from life and only denies the happiness and freedom of here and now.

Often you do not even know why you are in a hurry. It almost becomes a biological phenomenon to be in a rush. Wake up and become aware of the rush in you!

It is ridiculous to be in a rush to slow down. Just be aware of the rush and it will take care of itself. Slowing down does not mean procrastinating or being lethargic, though it is easy to be at the extremes of either rushing or lethargy. Rushing is caused by feverishness, and feverishness arises out of deficiency, a need to achieve. Dynamism is an expression of fulfillment. The golden rule is to be awake, and when you are awake you cannot help but be dynamic.

This moment realize that you are awake.

Gangtok, Sikkim, India
April 7, 2002

Creativity brings a new beginning to "time." When you are creative, you break the monotony of time. Everything becomes fresh and alive. Creativity brings along with it a new round of enthusiasm. Both creative and procreative impulses in nature are associated with enthusiasm. When you are enthusiastic, you are closer to the creative principle of existence.

Deep silence is the mother of creativity. No creativity can come out of one who is too busy, worried, over-ambitious or lethargic. Balanced activity, rest and yoga can kindle skills and creativity in you.

European Ashram, Bad Antogast, Germany
August 6, 2002

When people consider past events to be the result of free will they are filled with remorse and regret. When they consider future events as destiny, lethargy and inertia set in. A wise person will consider the past as destiny and the future as free will. When you consider the past as destiny, no more questions are raised and the mind is at ease. And when you consider the future as free will you are filled with enthusiasm and dynamism. Of course there will be some uncertainty and some anxiety when you consider the future as free will, but it can also bring alertness and creativity.

Question: How do we remove the anxiety?

By having faith in the Divine and doing sadhana.

Consider the past as destiny, the future as free will and the present moment as Divinity.

New Delhi, India
September 5, 2002

When someone said, "I have some property for you to consider as an ashram," Sri Sri answered, "I want every home to be an ashram."

How many of you consider your home to be an ashram? If not, what keeps your home from being an ashram? What are the impediments? What do you think are the qualities of an ashram?

Weggis, Switzerland
January 11, 1996

What is the difference between a tourist and a pilgrim?

Both are on a journey. Where a tourist satisfies the senses, a pilgrim is in quest of the truth. A tourist gets tired and tanned, while a pilgrim sparkles with spirit. Every move a pilgrim makes is done with sacredness and gratitude, while a tourist is often preoccupied and unaware.

A tourist compares his journey with other experiences and places, and thus is not in the present moment. But a pilgrim has a sense of sacredness so he tends to be in the present moment.

Most people in life are just tourists without even being aware of it. Only a few make their life a pilgrimage. Tourists come, look around, take pictures in their minds, only to come back again. But pilgrims are at home everywhere – they are hollow and empty.

When you consider life to be sacred, nature waits on you.

Are you a tourist or a pilgrim?

Jamshedpur, India
November 3, 2000

Those you associate with can either elevate you or pull you down. At first there is an attraction but then delusion. This keeps your mind swinging between the two extremes causing love and hatred. With the power of knowledge and satsang you can rise above this dilemma.

Bangalore Ashram, India
May 2, 1996

Normally in the world people with similar tendencies group together – intelligent people get together, fools get together, happy people get together, ambitious people get together and disgruntled people also get together to celebrate their problems.

Disgruntled people get together, they complain and pull each other down. Frustrated people cannot be with someone happy because the other is not dancing to their tune. You only feel comfortable when the other person is in tune with you. Intelligent people do not feel at home with foolish people. Foolish people feel that intelligent ones are not humane. People with wisdom feel at home with the disgruntled as well as the happy, foolish and intelligent. Similarly, people with all these tendencies feel at home with the wise.

Just turn around and look at what goes on in your group – are you grateful or grumbling? Take responsibility to uplift the people around you. That is Satsang, not just singing and leaving.

The wise person is like the sky where all birds fly.

Montreal Ashram, Quebec, Canada
July 17, 2002

Those who fight for their rights are weak for they do not know their inner strength, their magnanimity. The weaker you are, the more you demand your rights. Asserting your rights makes you isolated and poor. People who fight for their rights take pride in it. This is an ignorant pride. You need to recognize no one can take away your rights. They are yours.

The courageous will give away their rights. The degree to which you give away your rights indicates your freedom, your strength. The stronger you are the more you give away your rights. Only those who have their rights can give them away! Demanding rights does not really bring them to you, and in giving them away you do not really lose them.

- Poor are those who demand their rights.
- Richer are those who know their rights cannot be taken away.
- Richest are those who give away their rights.

- Demand for rights is ignorance, agony.
- Knowing no one can take away your rights is freedom.
- Giving away your rights is love, wisdom.

St. Louis, Missouri, United States
June 24, 1998

Honor reduces freedom. Your fame, honor and virtue can limit your freedom.

Nobody expects a good person to make a mistake, so the better you are, the higher the expectations people have of you. It is then that you lose your freedom. Your virtues and good actions are like a golden cage. You are trapped by your own good actions for everyone expects more from a good person. Nobody expects anything from a bad person.

Most people are stuck in this cage of prestige and honor. They cannot smile. They are constantly worried about keeping their prestige and their honor; it becomes more important than their own life. Just being good or doing good to retain prestige and honor is worthless. Prestige and honor can bring more misery in life than poverty.

Many desire fame, but little do they know that they are looking for a cage.

It is an art to be dignified and yet not be suffocated by it. Only the wise know this. For the wise one it is natural to be honorable, but he has no concerns even if it is lost. Despite having fame or prestige, he will live as though he has none. A wise person can handle any fame without feeling suffocated.

By doing good in society you can gain prestige, then when you enjoy the prestige and honor your freedom is lost.

Question: Then how do you keep your freedom?

By being like a child, by considering the world a dream, a burden or a joke.

Panama City, Panama
May 3, 2001

Life moves by dual factors – inner tendencies and outer influences.

Inner tendencies form your attitudes and behavior, while external influences make strong impressions in your mind. Your tendencies often generate external situations, and situations around you can form tendencies within you. This is called karma. Both these factors – the tendencies from within and influences from outside can be either beneficial or harmful.

It is awareness that filters the outer negative influences and it is awareness that corrects and annihilates the unhealthy inner tendencies. This awareness is called gyana. The purpose of education is to develop this awareness so that you can be selective about your tendencies and influences.

It is practically impossible to resist the external influences and the inner tendencies without raising one's consciousness. This can be gradual or sudden.

This is how a human being has both free will and destiny. Freedom is when you have a say about your tendencies and your influences, but only awareness and impeccable devotion can bring this freedom.

Stockholm, Sweden
June 20, 2001

Nigraha means control.
Agraha means insistence.
Satyagraha means steadfast determination.
Duragraha means blind adamancy, reckless stubbornness.

These four allow you to progress when practiced for just a limited period of time and will give limited results, positive or negative. But if practiced for a long period of time, they will eat away the potential of life. You have to transcend all four to attain peace.

Freedom is when you transcend all four – control, insistence, determination and adamancy. They are inevitable to streamline life, but you need to transcend them to be free.

Washington, D.C., United States
July 3, 2002

When you follow fun, misery follows you.
When you follow knowledge, fun follows you.

Jakarta, Indonesia
April 10, 1996

Words have meanings that we distort. For example, the word "brainwashing" implies that your brain sometimes needs washing. You do not want to walk around with a dirty brain, a dirty mind. What is wrong with the word "brainwashing?" It indicates a clean brain, a clean mind, but it is used in a derogatory manner.

The word "disillusioned" is the same. It is good that you are disillusioned; it means you have come to reality. Purana means "that which is new in town, the most modern" but it is now used in the sense of being old. The word "enthused" comes from the Greek which means "God is with us." Then it came to mean crazy, and today it has changed again. In the course of time, meanings of words change.

Do not be stuck on words. Your worries are words. Your ideas are words. Wisdom is beyond words. It is the very Being. It is the essence of all words. See and relate beyond words. Then there are no lies in your life.

If you manipulate words, it is a lie. If you play on words, it is a joke. If you rely on words, it is ignorance. If you transcend words, it is wisdom.

Bali Cliff Resort, Indonesia
April 18, 1996

What shall we talk about today? What is the point in talking about something of which you know nothing? There is no point in talking about what you know and no point in talking about what you do not know.

There is no end to learning but there is an end to unlearning. That is when you become totally hollow and empty.

European Ashram, Germany
June 5, 1996

Sri Sri was walking along the beach with some devotees near a huge desalination plant that converted salt water to fresh water. Nearby was a coconut tree. Sri Sri pointed out that the tree is a natural desalination plant. It takes salt water from the earth and makes fresh water inside the coconut. Knowledge is like that tree – it takes us from salty mud to pure bliss.

Dallas, Texas, United States
January 22, 1997

Knowledge will be different at different levels of consciousness. At a particular level of consciousness you will achieve anasuya which is a state of mind that is devoid of fault-finding eyes. If a mirror is dusty, you need to clean it. But if your eyes have cataracts, any amount of dusting the mirror will not help. First you have to remove the cataracts, then you can see that the mirror is clean.

There is a type of mindset that always finds fault, even in the best of conditions. Even when people with this mindset have the best, they still find faults. With the best possible companion, or the most beautiful painting, they will still find something wrong. That kind of mindset cannot know sacred knowledge. Krishna tells Arjuna that he is giving him a royal secret because he achieved the state of anasuya. "You find no fault in me even though you are so close."

From a distance, even craters cannot be seen, and even on a smooth surface there will be holes. If you are only interested in the holes, you will not see the magnanimity of things. If you are not in anasuya, knowledge cannot blossom and there is no point in giving knowledge to you.

Question: What about discrimination – wisdom?

If it is in your vision, your perception, then you will find discrimination. The moment you are off the path, everything will be wrong. That is not anasuya. For example, after ten years of friendship you no longer see the good in that relationship; you only find faults. However, once you discover you have the wrong vision – you have discovered your cataracts – then half of the problem disappears. There is a fine line here. Instead of saying, "My vision is blurred," you say, "The whole world is not sharp." Suppose someone is coming through a door but it is windy, so you shut the door. If the person thinks the door has been slammed in his face, then this is asuya, not anasuya. Most people are like this.

Asuya is finding fault. It is seeing malicious intent everywhere. It is like a child who says, "Mother, you do not love me!" The child's vision is wrong. If a mother does not love her child, who will? It is the same when someone comes and says, "Guruji, you do not love me!" If I do not love him, then nobody else in the world will. Where else will they find love? Nowhere. A mother may get frustrated but not a master.

Question: Can a person achieve anasuya without being enlightened?

Not always. This is an excuse. To find enlightenment, you must have this vision.

London, United Kingdom
August 24, 1995

Knowledge must be digested properly, and an inability to do so causes:

- False ego, which has no cure.
- Disinterest, taking things for granted, lack of awareness.
- Familiarity without understanding, without depth – shallowness.
- A tendency to preach.
- "Heart" burn.
- Using knowledge for one's own small ends.
- Adamancy, stubbornness.

If you are in love with the Divine, then you can digest knowledge. Love is the appetizer, knowledge is the main course and seva is the exercise. Without love and seva, knowledge becomes indigestible.

Los Angeles, California, United States
January 30, 1997

To be able to know yourself or to judge your actions, you need to understand tarka, vitarka and kutarka.

Kutarka is wrong logic. Most people use this logic and get caught up in ignorance. For example, the door is half open means the door is half closed. Therefore, when the door is fully open means the door is fully closed. Another example – God is love. Love is blind. Therefore God is blind.

Tarka is sequential logical understanding which increases scientific knowledge. When sequential logical understanding changes, then scientific conclusions change. For example, pesticides and antibiotics were considered to be very useful and harmless, but they are now proven to be harmful. In tarka, paradigms change.

Vitarka is asking questions to which there are no evident answers such as "Who am I?" "Where am I?" "What do I really want?" These philosophical questions bring forth spiritual knowledge, increase your awareness and bring about the blossoming of consciousness. Atma gyan increases.

The wise know how to distinguish between these three. They will not apply kutarka or tarka for vitarka, or use vitarka for tarka.

Bangalore Ashram, India
April 9, 1998

When a materialistic person tells you a secret, it only creates doubt and spreads malaise. When a wise or spiritual person tells you a secret, it uplifts your consciousness and spreads benevolence.

Bangalore Ashram, India
October 7, 2000

A wise person makes no effort to conceal a secret, but he does not make an effort to reveal a secret either. For example, you do not talk about menstruation or death to a five-year-old, but as they grow older these things are not hidden from them. They become known as a matter of course.

An unenlightened person tries to protect a secret, or he reveals a secret at the wrong time, to the wrong person, or in the wrong place. And he makes a big fuss about secrets. Trying to protect a secret causes anxiety and discomfort.

An ignorant one is not comfortable with a secret, whether revealed or unrevealed, but the wise one is comfortable with a secret, whether revealed or unrevealed.

Bangalore Ashram, India
December 16, 1999

A person who argues should not be given knowledge. An argumentative mind is not receptive to knowledge. When someone is in an argumentative mood, then giving knowledge or advice is in vain. A person in an argumentative mood feels he knows it all, so he is not ready for knowledge. That is why wise people do not give advice when they are in an argumentative environment.

Argument has a purpose. It can bring out the truth if there is no emotion or sense of "I" attached to it. Argument can also have a disadvantage. It can make untruth appear to be truth. A wise man will not take arguments seriously; he will just have fun with them. Wisdom is beyond all arguments.

Lake Tahoe, California, United States
July 12, 2000

There are two types of knowledge. The first one is pure knowledge and the second one is applied knowledge. Applied knowledge may benefit you immediately and directly, but pure knowledge benefits you indirectly in the long run.

If there are some things that you have studied or understood which you are unable to put into practice, do not get disheartened. Sometime in the future, if you do not discard as impractical the knowledge you have, it will be of use to you.

Often people discard pure knowledge for its lack of immediate application. In fact these two types of knowledge complement each other. Applied knowledge without pure knowledge remains weak. And pure knowledge without application will remain unfulfilled. Do not discard or label knowledge as impractical, and do not label yourself as weak or unworthy because you are unable to apply the knowledge in your day-to-day life.

Sometimes when you are alone in nature, silent, taking a walk, looking at the sand on the beach, a bird in the sky, or while meditating – suddenly knowledge will emerge and you will recognize knowledge dawning in your life.

Palo Alto, California, United States
May 11, 2002

The purpose of technology is to harness nature to bring information and comfort to human beings. When spiritual values – human values – are ignored and neglected, technology brings fear and destruction instead of comfort.

Technology without human values considers nature a dead object. Science gives insight into the life of nature and spirituality makes nature come alive. In the eyes of children there is nothing dead in the world – animals, trees, the sun and the moon – they all have life, they all have emotions, they all have feelings. But in the eyes of a stressed and ignorant person, even human beings are like robots – objects.

Technology without spirituality is destructive. Spirituality is the technology of consciousness and the whole world is the play and display of consciousness.

European Ashram, Bad Antogast, Germany
August 3, 2000

Often business is looked down upon by spiritual people, and spirituality is considered impractical by businessmen. The ancient people realized that spirituality is the heart and business is the legs. An individual or a society is incomplete without both these aspects. Business brings material comfort and spirituality brings mental and emotional comfort. Spirituality brings ethics and fair practice to business.

In the mind-body complex, depriving either the body or the mind of comfort means depriving both of them. You cannot talk of spirituality to the poorest of poor people without taking care of their basic needs. They need to be supported materially. There is no spirituality in the world that is devoid of service and service cannot happen if material needs are ignored. Service cannot happen only through the lips; it needs legs to work.

Every system has its flaws. Capitalism exploits the poor while socialism dampens individual creativity and the entrepreneurial spirit. Spirituality is the bridge between socialism and capitalism. Spirituality gives to capitalists the heart to serve and to socialists the spirit to innovate.

New York City, New York, United States
February 2, 2002

Communism has three goals: to check the greed of feudal and capitalist societies, to halt the fanaticism and fundamentalism of religious communities, and to care for the needy and share resources with them.

- Only spirituality brings fulfillment to communism.
- Only spirituality checks greed and opens the hearts of the wealthy to help the needy.
- Only spirituality stops the fanaticism and fundamentalism of religious groups and creates a sense of belongingness with the whole world.
- Only spirituality cultures caring and sharing.
- Only spirituality brings about open-mindedness and a progressive attitude.

Communism cannot fulfill its goals without spirituality. It is impossible and time has proved it. Spirituality nourishes communism.

Bangalore Ashram, India
April 16, 2002

Do not feel shy to speak about human and spiritual values. The time has come now to call the whole world to these principles.

The All is calling,
The ball is rolling,
Time is milling,
The soul is willing...

European Ashram, Bad Antogast, Germany
New Years Eve, 1997

Sri Sri was on the porch with a group of people when he sent Kashi to get sweets from inside his home, but Kashi returned saying he could not find them. He went again and again, three times, and still he could not find them. Then Sri Sri went in and came out with the sweets and gave them to everyone.

This is exactly what happens in life. Many want sweetness in life. Some are searching hard, but only one finds it. And when that one finds it, he gives it to everyone.

Bangalore Ashram, India
December 7, 1999

The main reasons to be with a guru are:

- You want to have your wishes fulfilled.
- You find it more pleasurable.
- You come for comfort as everything else is more painful to you.
- You want to evolve and become enlightened; you want to attain higher knowledge.
- You have a vision or a goal in common with a guru, whom you see as a missionary or visionary, who can help you achieve your goal.
- You are there just to serve and to give comfort.
- You belong to your guru. You have no choice.

European Ashram, Bad Antogast, Germany
January 12, 2000

In the Orient, having a master is considered a matter of pride. A master is a symbol of security, love and a sign of great wealth. Being with a guru is like being with one's higher Self. Not having a master was looked down upon as a sign of misfortune. Orphans were not those without parents; rather those without a master were considered orphans. In the Occident having a master is considered shameful and a sign of weakness, for there masters are thought to enslave people.

In the Orient, people take pride in having a guru for every aspect of life – a religious guru – dharmaguru, a family guru – kulaguru, a guru for the kingdom – rajguru, a guru for a particular discipline – vidyaguru, and a spiritual guru – satguru.

In the Orient, masters make their disciples feel powerful, while in the Occident, masters are thought to make people weak. In the Occident, a master is considered a motivator and one who provokes competition. In the Orient, masters give a deep sense of belongingness that enables people to dissolve their limited identity into infinity.

European Ashram, Bad Antogast, Germany
August 9, 2001

Is your guru responsible for your enlightenment? If yes and you are not awakened, then he is to be blamed. If you find freedom, then your guru is again to be blamed because he has been partial to you. If your guru can set you free, then he can do it to the whole world. So your guru is not responsible for your awakening, and yet freedom is next to impossible without having a guru.

So a guru is responsible and yet not responsible. This is a mystery.

Bangalore Ashram, India
May 25, 2000

A student's job is to satisfy his spiritual master, but how can you satisfy someone who is already satisfied? If your guru is satisfied, then your growth is slowed, but if your guru is unsatisfied, he is away from the Self.

If your guru is satisfied, then what can inspire you to grow? If he is unsatisfied, he cannot be a guru. And if he is satisfied, he cannot be a guru!

So what is the answer?

Ljubljana, Slovenia
January 16, 1996

A guru is nothing but wisdom and love. He is that principle which is wisdom and love, which is awakened in each one who has stepped onto the path. He is also that person in whom there is no gap between life, wisdom and love.

Often one recognizes wisdom but sees a gap between wisdom and one's own life. The purpose of becoming a disciple of a guru is to bridge that gap.

Being with a guru means spontaneous integration of life and wisdom.

Lake Tahoe, California, United States
Guru Purnima, July 28, 1999

Chapter Three

You, God and Beyond

Abiding in the Self you become the valentine for the whole world. Spirit is the valentine of the material world, and the material world is the valentine of the spirit. They are made for each other. They uphold each other. If you clutch onto material objects and do not respect the spirit, then the material world will be displeased. If you honor the spirit, then you will care for the world, and when you care for the world, it will take care of you.

London, United Kingdom
February 14, 1996

An ignorant person either disbelieves or believes what an individual says, but the wise one does neither. His faith rests on Kala, or time. When the time is good, a foe will behave like a friend. When the time is not good, even a friend will behave like a foe. An ignorant person disbelieves in both time and the Divine beyond time, while the wise one believes in Mahakala – the Grand Time, or Shiva.

In the world and in time there is always room for improvement. You can improve your time and your nature. Only Being is perfect all the time. Take refuge in Being and become immutable.

Know that "I am" immutable.

Bus on the Tour-de-France
June 3, 1997

All sensory pleasures in the world are like wrapping paper; the true bliss is the present inside. Divine love is the present, yet we are holding onto the paper believing we have already enjoyed the gift. It is like putting a chocolate inside your mouth with the paper still on. A little chocolate may seep into your mouth, but the wrapper causes discomfort.

Unwrap the present. The whole world is there for you to enjoy. The wise know how to enjoy the gift inside, while the ignorant get stuck with the paper.

Weggis, Switzerland
January 11, 1996

Deep rest is bliss, and bliss is the understanding that only God exists. Knowing that only God exists is the deepest rest possible.

This conviction or experience that "only God exists" is samadhi. Samadhi is the mother of all talents, strengths and virtues. Samadhi is needed even for the most materialistic person because a materialistic person seeks to gain strength and virtues. To be in samadhi, you do not need any effort or talents, strengths or virtues.

Withdrawing from all types of physical and mental activity is rest. That is built into our system as sleep, and sleep is the best friend of activity. Samadhi is conscious rest. Samadhi is the best friend of life. To be alive in your full potential, samadhi is indispensable.

Restlessness obstructs samadhi. What is restlessness and what are the remedies?

Berlin, Germany
June 7, 2001

There are five types of restlessness.

The first type of restlessness is caused by a particular place. When you move away from that place – the street or the house – you immediately feel better. Chanting, singing, laughing and children playing can change this atmospheric restlessness. If you chant and sing, the vibration in the place changes.

The second type of restlessness is in the body. Eating the wrong food, eating vata-aggravating food, eating at odd times, not exercising and overworking can all cause physical restlessness. The remedy for this is exercise, moderation in work habits and going on a vegetable or juice diet for one or two days.

The third type of restlessness is mental restlessness. It is caused by ambition, strong thoughts, likes or dislikes. Only knowledge can cure this restlessness – seeing life from a broader perspective, having knowledge of the Self and awareness of the impermanence of everything around you. If you achieve everything, so what? After your achievement, you will die. Knowledge of your death and life, confidence in the Self and confidence in the Divine all calm down mental restlessness.

The fourth type is emotional restlessness. Any amount of knowledge cannot help here – only Kriya helps. With Kriya, all emotional restlessness vanishes. The presence of your guru, a wise person, or a saint will also help to calm your emotional restlessness.

The final type of restlessness is rare. It is the restlessness of the soul. When everything feels empty and meaningless, know you are very fortunate. That longing is the restlessness of the soul. Do not try to get rid of it – embrace it, welcome it. People do all sorts of things to get rid of it – they change places, jobs, or partners, they do this, they do that. It seems to help for some time, but it does not last.

Only this restlessness of the soul can bring authentic prayer in you. It brings perfection, siddhis and miracles in life. It is so precious to get that innermost longing for the Divine. Satsang and the presence of an enlightened one soothe the restlessness of the soul.

European Ashram, Bad Antogast, Germany
June 14, 2001

When your mind is not complaining and is responsible, courageous, confident and hollow and empty, you are inexplicably beautiful. A person who cannot correct or act on a complaint has no right to complain. And a person who can correct or act on a complaint, will never complain. Complaining is a sign of weakness. Complaining is the nature of utter ignorance where one does not know the Self. Complaints take away the beauty that is inborn in you, and the effects show up more clearly for those on this path.

The worldly mind is a complaining mind; the divine mind is a dancing mind. Just complaining without looking for a solution is irresponsibility. And when solutions do not work, finding alternative solutions is courage.

For external beauty, you put on things; for real beauty, you have to drop all those things. For external beauty you have to have make up; for real beauty you only have to realize that you are made up.

Bangalore Ashram, India
April 30, 1997

There is a place you can come where everything is beautiful. Tourists go from place to place looking for beauty, and they try to take away the beauty. They only get tired and tanned. Yet the most beautiful spot anywhere is right here. When you come here, you find that wherever you are, everything is so beautiful.

Where is this place? Do not look here and there. Where do you go? Within you. When you come here, then any place is beautiful. Then wherever you go, you add beauty.

If you are unhappy, sweet things are nauseating, music is disturbing, and even the moon is irritating. When you are calm and centered, clouds are magical, rain is liquid sunshine, and even noise is musical.

Book yourself on a trip to this most beautiful place in the universe. Then you will find that every day is a vacation and a celebration.

Honolulu, Hawaii, United States
February 1, 1996

It is difficult to see God as formless and it is difficult to see God as having a form. The formless is so abstract and God in a form appears to be too limited so some people prefer to be atheists.

Atheism is not a reality; it is just a matter of convenience. When you have a spirit of inquiry or when you search for truth, atheism falls apart. With a spirit of inquiry, you cannot deny something that you cannot disprove. An atheist denies God without first disproving God's existence. In order to disprove God, you must have enormous knowledge and when you have enormous knowledge, you cannot disprove it.

To say that something does not exist, you must know about the whole universe. So you can never be one hundred percent atheistic. An atheist is only a believer who is sleeping.

For a person to say, "I don't believe in anything," means he must believe in himself so he believes in a self that he does not even know.

An atheist can never be sincere because sincerity needs depth and an atheist refuses to go to his depth. The deeper he goes, he finds a void, a field of all possibilities, and he has to accept that there are many secrets he does not know. He would then need to acknowledge his ignorance – which he refuses to do – because the moment he is sincere, he seriously starts doubting his atheism. A doubt-free atheist is nearly impossible. An atheist can never be sincere and doubt-free.

When an atheist realizes his ignorance, what does he do? Where does he go? Does he go to a guru? What does a guru do to him?

Bangalore Ashram, India
December 15, 2000

An atheist does not believe in either values or in the abstract. When an atheist comes to the guru, what happens? He starts experiencing his own form and discovers that he is indeed formless, hollow and empty, and this abstract non-form becomes more and more concrete.

A guru makes the abstract more real, and what you thought was solid appears more unreal. Sensitivity and subtlety dawn. Perception of love – not as an emotion, but as the substratum of existence – becomes evident. The formless spirit shines through every form in creation and the mystery of life deepens, shattering atheism. Then the journey begins; it is a journey with four stages.

The first stage is saarupya – to see the formless in the form – seeing God in all forms. Often, one feels more comfortable seeing God as formless rather than having a form, because with a form, one feels a distance, a duality, a fear of rejection and other limitations. Other than in deep sleep or in samadhi, all of our interactions in life are with a form. If you do not see God as having a form, then the waking part of life remains devoid of the Divine.

All those who accept God to be formless use symbols and perhaps love the symbols more than God Himself. If God comes to a Christian and tells him to leave the cross, or if God tells a Muslim to drop the crescent, he may not do it. Initially, loving the formless is possible only through forms.

The second stage is saamipya – closeness – feeling absolutely close to the form you have chosen and reaching out to the formless. This leads to a sense of intimacy with all of creation. In this stage, one overcomes the fear of rejection and other fears, but this stage remains bound by time and space.

The third stage is saanidhya – feeling the presence of the Divine by which you transcend the limitations of time and space.

The final stage is saayujya – when you are firmly entrenched in the Divine. It is then you realize you are one with the Divine. There is a total merging with the Beloved and all duality disappears.

This is that and that is this.

Question: Does a believer also go through these four stages?

Certainly. Both an atheist and a believer go through the four stages.

European Ashram, Bad Antogast, Germany
December 25, 2000

A pure atheist is impossible to find. An atheist is one who believes only in the concrete and tangible, but life is not all concrete and tangible, nor is this universe. Whether it is business, science or art, all involve a certain amount of guesswork, assumptions, imagination and intuition. All of them have some aspects that are abstract in nature and are not tangible. The moment an atheist accepts, even remotely, something that is unexplainable, he ceases to be an atheist. An intelligent person cannot rule out all the mysteries in life and the universe, and hence cannot honestly be an atheist. So-called atheists are perhaps only denouncing certain concepts of God.

Question: Was Buddha an atheist?

No in one sense because he professed emptiness, which is very hard for an atheist to accept, and yes in another sense because he did not profess concepts of God.

An atheist believes only what he can see, but Buddha said all that you see is not real. If only all present-day atheists could be Buddhas!

Bangalore Ashram, India
April 17, 2002

There is a Big Mind and a small mind. Sometimes the Big Mind wins over the small mind and sometimes it is the other way around. When the small mind wins, it causes misery and when the Big Mind wins, it is joy. The small mind promises joy but leaves you empty-handed. You may initially be resistant to the Big Mind but it will fill you with joy.

The word guru means great. Jaya means victory. Deva means one who is fun-loving, playful, light. Some who are playful are often not dignified, and those who are dignified are often not playful. Jai Guru Dev means victory to the Big Mind in you that is both dignified and playful. Jai Guru Dev means "Victory to the greatness in you."

You do not say victory to the master as he has already achieved the Big Mind. You say victory to your own Self, your own Big Mind, which is being protested by the small mind.

Bangalore Ashram, India
September 27, 1995

Buddha was enlightened under the Bodhi tree. He then stood up and watched the tree from a distance for seven days. He took sixteen steps towards the tree and under each step blossomed a lotus flower. This is the legend.

The Bodhi tree is symbolic of both sansara (the world) and dharma. The lotus flower symbolizes clarity, dispassion, love, beauty and purity.

It is only when you are detached in life that you can watch the sansara and all of its plays. When you witness the sansara, every step you take is benevolent and impeccable. When every action of yours is preceded by witnessing, then every move you make in this sansara becomes perfect and significant.

Bodh Gaya, India
November 9, 2000

If you think you are ignorant, you know who you are.

- And if you know who you are, you are enlightened.
- And if you are enlightened, then you certainly are not ignorant.
- If you think you are intelligent, then you do not know who you are.
- And if do not know who you are, then you really are ignorant!

It is better to realize your ignorance, and be enlightened!

European Ashram, Bad Antogast, Germany
May 20, 1999

Once every 12 years, all the seers, saints and aspirants of spiritual knowledge congregate at the confluence, or sangam, of the three holy rivers – Ganga, Yamuna and Saraswati. The Ganga is a symbol of knowledge and self-inquiry. It is on the banks of the Yamuna that events of love have been immortalized. When knowledge and love come together, when the head meets the heart, Saraswati, symbolic of wisdom and the fine arts, emerges.

When a tiny atom explodes, the radiation lasts for a long time. The mind is more subtle than one millionth of an atom. When the mind explodes, that is enlightenment.

Over the centuries, thousands of sages who have meditated, done penance and have been enlightened come to the Kumbha Mela and relieve themselves of the burden of the merits gained through Sadhana by bathing in the rivers. The water can absorb the energy that they radiate. The seekers, who come from all corners to be in the company of seers and saints, gain that merit when they take a dip in the rivers.

Space by itself cannot be bought and a lump of clay has no value, but when space is enveloped by clay it gains value, this is a kumbha – a pot. Spirit is everywhere in nature, but when it dawns in the human body as an elevated state of consciousness, then it gains immense value. An embodied and elevated spirit is usually referred to as kumbha. This is why the enlightened age is also called the Aquarian age. Kumbha denotes a pot, which is symbolic of fullness and perfection.

New Delhi, India
January 26, 2001

The foolish one uses spiritual power to gain material comfort.

An intelligent one uses the material world to rise high in the spirit.

When you transcend the intellect, you allow yourself to be used by the spirit.

One who is awake neither uses anything nor loses anything.

Become intelligent – transcend and wake up.

At an undisclosed location in the United States
July 11, 2002

The lord of the diverse universe is called Ganesha.

The whole universe is nothing but clusters of atoms – groups of qualities, of energy. Gana means group and a group cannot exist without a "lord." Like the queen bee whose mere existence brings forth the honeycomb, this diverse universe in itself is enough evidence for Ganesha's presence.

Ganesha, or lord, was born from the unmanifest transcendental consciousness, the Self, called Shiva. Just as when atoms bond and matter comes into existence, so when all the fragmented aspects of human consciousness bond, Divinity happens effortlessly and that is the birth of Ganesha from Shiva.

Bangalore Ashram, India
August 23, 2001

What is Maya?

Maya is that which can be measured. The whole world can be measured, that is why it is Maya. All five elements – earth, water, fire, air and ether – can all be measured.

Question: Can space be measured?

Only in space can things be measured. Space is the first dimension of measurement.

Measurement is always relative and not absolute. For example, if something weighs six pounds on earth, it will weigh only one pound on the moon. The light of the star you see today is not really today's light. It has taken at least four years for the light to reach you. Both size and weight change in air, water and earth. So "measure" is illusory and not dependable. Your bones, skin, body, environment and the five elements can be measured; you can put a value, a quantity, to them. So, the whole world is Maya. All measurements only provide a relative understanding. Einstein's theory of relativity correlates with the Advaita (non-dual) philosophy.

But what is not Maya? Everything that cannot be measured is not Maya. You cannot say one ounce of love, two ounces of peace and five kilograms of happiness. Can you be measured? It is not possible. Your body has weight, but not you. Truth cannot be measured, ananda – or joy – cannot be measured, and beauty cannot be measured. All these are part of consciousness or easwara – the Divine – and are called Mayi.

Bangalore Ashram, India
December 21, 2001

Man has a tendency to own things. When he owns something small, his mind stays small, his life gets stifled and his whole consciousness is immersed in his house, his car, his spouse, his children and so on. A recluse leaves his home and goes far away. But there he starts owning his asana, his rosary, his books, his concepts and his knowledge.

Ownership has simply shifted from objects and people to ideas and practices. But a wise one knows that he owns the sun, the moon, the stars, the air, all of space and the Divine in its entirety. When you own something big, then your consciousness also expands, and when you own something small, then small negative emotions, such as anger and greed, start to rise.

I wonder why people do not feel connected to the sun? The very existence of life depends upon the sun. Perhaps it is lack of awareness that causes people to refuse to acknowledge and own their connectedness to the macrocosmic universe. The rishis in ancient India, the Native Americans and aboriginals from all over the globe have insisted that you can feel connected to the sun, the moon and the directions.

When you own something magnanimous, your consciousness also becomes magnanimous.

Bangalore Ashram, India
September 13, 2001

At their wedding anniversary, a couple devoted to Sri Sri presented an ornate fan to him, saying, "A fan from two grateful fans."

At this Sri Sri said, "Devotees are the fan; God is the air. The air is always there, but the fan makes you feel it. God is always there, but devotees make His presence felt!"

Bangalore Ashram, India
September 9, 1999

Guruji held up a pistachio nut and asked, "What is this?" Everybody said, "A pistachio." Guruji held up a pistachio nut without the shell and asked, "What is this?" Everybody said, "A pistachio." Guruji then held up the shell and asked, "What is this?" Everybody said, "A shell."

As the nut with or without the shell is pistachio, similarly spirit with or without the body is God. But just as the shell without the nut is not a pistachio, the body without spirit is not God. Spirit is certainly God because it is present everywhere. The body is certainly not God because it is not present everywhere.

God is within the body and God embodies the whole universe. Those who have eyes will see. When asked, "Are you God?" to whom is the question addressed? As it is only the spirit that answers, you have no choice but to say, "Yes!"

Bali, Indonesia
April 5, 2001

It was thought that saying "I am God" is blasphemy. I tell you, to say "I am not God" is blasphemy. When you say "I am not God," you deny God His omnipresence.

You are made up of love. If you say "I am not God," you are denying that God is love. If you are love and you say "I am not God," you are saying God is not love, and that is blasphemy.

"I am" is your consciousness. If you say "I am not God," you deny that God is aware, alert and awake. You exist. When you say "I am not God," you deny God a portion of existence and that is blasphemy. You are denying the scriptures that say "God made man in His own image." If you say "I am not God," you are denying God.

Question: If God is omnipresent, why is there hatred and suffering in this world?

Just as in a movie, when light passes through the film, it does not matter to the light what the film portrays. Tragedy or comedy, hero or villain, the light is always there. In the Absolute there are no opposites. All opposites are part of relative existence.

Relative existence is not the complete picture. Good and bad, right and wrong, everything is relative. Milk is good, but too much milk can kill you. A drop of poison can save a life, but most medicines are poisonous if taken in the wrong dose. These are neither absolutely good nor bad; they just are.

Truth transcends duality, and God is the absolute and only truth. In the same way, no matter what is happening in your mind, you are God.

Kannur, Kerala, India
December 10, 2000

A lady commented to Sri Sri, "I want an honest and humble man in my life."

I am neither honest nor humble! I cannot tell everyone that I am God, as not everyone will understand. So I am not honest. I am not humble – how can God be humble?

If I am humble, I am not honest.
If I am honest, I cannot be humble.

Halifax, Nova Scotia, Canada
June 22, 2000

Longing itself is Divine.
Longing for worldly things makes you inert.
Longing for infinity fills you with life.

When longing dies, inertia sets in. But longing also brings a sense of pain. To avoid the pain, you try to push away the longing. The skill is to bear the pain of longing and move on. Do not try to find a shortcut to overcome longing. Do not make the longing short – that's why it is called loooonging.

True longing in itself brings up moments of bliss. That is why in ancient days longing was kept alive by singing and listening to kathas, or stories.

When longing transcends relationships, then judgments, jealousy and all negative feelings drop. It is only with wisdom and self-knowledge that you can transcend relationships. People often think wisdom is devoid of longing – no! Such wisdom is dry. The longing that comes with true wisdom makes life juicier. The Divine is certainly juicy!

Longing gives you the power to bless. Bless the entire creation for the longing in you is God.

Bangalore Ashram, India
February 8, 2001

In all cultures throughout the ages, certain places, times of the year, persons and symbols have been considered sacred.

Native Americans and other tribal people consider the earth, sun, moon and all the directions to be sacred. In the ancient tradition of India, the rishis considered all the rivers, mountains and even animals, trees and herbs to be sacred.

And what of people? They are definitely sacred. Various cultures honor certain people and consider them to be sacred.

For Christians, the cross, Jerusalem, Christmas and the Pope are sacred. For Muslims, the crescent moon, Mecca and the month of Ramadan are sacred. The Hindus consider the river Ganges, the Himalayas and the Swamis to be sacred.

When you consider a place, time, person, symbol, or act sacred, your attention is undivided and whole. When things are ordinary and the same, you tend to slip into unawareness and inertia. The moment you consider something sacred, your inertia disappears and you become more alive.

There is nothing as fulfilling as a sacred act. You put your heart and soul into a sacred act. When every action of yours becomes sacred, you have become one with the Divine. Then every minute of your life is sacred, every place you go to becomes sacred, every act of yours is sacred and every person you meet is only your reflection.

Question: Why does an act when performed repeatedly lose it sacredness?

This happens when your memory overpowers your consciousness and you lose your sensitivity. For example, people living in Benares do not feel that it is a sacred place. It is too familiar; that sensitivity is just not there.

Question: How can we preserve that feeling of sacredness in our acts?

Through living in the present moment and through sadhana. Your sadhana will not allow your memory to overpower consciousness. Then repetition is not a hindrance.

It is good to feel that some places, times, people and symbols are sacred so that you can be awake and alive. But eventually you need to transcend and feel that the entire creation and your whole life are sacred. For the person of God, the whole world, with all its symbols, places and people are sacred at all times.

Be a person of God!

European Ashram, Bad Antogast, Germany
December 1, 2000

Let the wind that blows be sweet
Let the oceans flow honey
Let all the herbs and plant kingdom be favorable to us
Let the nights be sweet and let the days be sweet
Let the dust of this planet be sweet to us
Let the heavens and our forefathers be sweet to us
Let all the trees be laden with honey
Let the Sun be sweet to us and let
all the radiations be favorable
Let all the animals be sweet to us
Let our food be favorable to us
Let all our thoughts and our speech
be sweet like honey
Let our life be pure and divine
Let it be sweet like honey.

Our human body is made to bring heaven on this earth, it is meant to bring sweetness into this world, not to spill venom.

It is easy to disparage someone, but it takes some guts, some intelligence, some courage to uplift people, to bring out the Divine quality in those around you. By bringing out Divine qualities in others, you will see the Divinity deep inside you.

Just as a lit candle can light another candle, only one who has can give.

One who is free can free you, one who is love can kindle love.

Sri Sri Ravi Shankar

The Art of Living
&
The International Association for Human Values

Transforming Lives

The Founder
His Holiness Sri Sri Ravi Shankar

His Holiness Sri Sri Ravi Shankar is a universally revered spiritual and humanitarian leader. His vision of a violence-free, stress-free society through the reawakening of human values has inspired millions to broaden their spheres of responsibility and work towards the betterment of the world.

Born in 1956 in southern India, Sri Sri was often found deep in meditation as a child. At the age of four, astonishes his teachers by reciting the Bhagavad Gita, an ancient Sanskrit scripture. He has always had the unique gift of presenting the deepest truths in the simplest of words.

Sri Sri established the Art of Living, an educational and humanitarian Non-Governmental Organisation that works in special consultative status with the Economic and Social Council (ECOSOC) of the United Nations in 1981. Present in over 140 countries, it formulates and implements lasting solutions to conflicts and issues faced by individuals, communities and nations. In 1997, he founded the International Association for Human Values (IAHV) to foster human values and lead sustainable development projects.

Sri Sri has reached out to an estimated 300 million people worldwide through personal interactions, public events, teachings, Art of Living workshops and humanitarian initiatives. He has brought to the masses ancient practices which were traditionally kept exclusive, and has designed many self-development techniques which can easily be integrated into daily life to calm the mind and instill confidence and enthusiasm. One of Sri Sri's most unique offerings to the world is the Sudarshan Kriya, a powerful breathing technique that facilitates physical, mental, emotional and social well-being.

Numerous honours have been bestowed upon Sri Sri, including the Order of the Pole Star (the highest state honour in Mongolia), the Peter the Great Award (Russian Federation), the Sant Shri Dnyaneshwara World Peace Prize (India) and the Global Humanitarian Award (USA). Sri Sri has addressed several international forums, including the United Nations Millennium World Peace Summit (2000), the World Economic Forum (2001, 2003) and several parliaments across the globe.

The Art of Living
In Service Around The World

(www.artofliving.org)

The largest volunteer-based network in the world, with a wide range of social, cultural and spiritual activities, the Art of Living has reached out to over 20 million people from all walks of life, since 1982. A non-profit, educational, humanitarian organization, it is committed to creating peace from the level of the individual upwards, and fostering human values within the global community. Currently, the Art of Living service projects and educational programmes are carried out in over 140 countries. The organisation works in special consultative status with the Economic and Social Council (ECOSOC) of the United Nations, participating in a variety of committees and activities related to health and conflict resolution.

The Art of Living Stress Elimination Programmes

Holistic Development of Body, Mind & Spirit

The Art of Living programmes are a combination of the best of ancient wisdom and modern science. They cater to every age group - children, youth, adults -and every section of society – rural communities, governments, corporate houses, etc. Emphasizing holistic living and personal self-development, the programmes facilitate the complete blossoming of an individual's full potential. The cornerstone of all our workshops is the Sudarshan Kriya, a unique, potent breathing practice.

- The Art of Living Course Part I
- The Art of Living Course Part II
- Sahaj Samadhi Meditation
- Divya Samaaj ka Nirmaan (DSN)
- The All Round Training in Excellence (ART Excel)
- The Youth Empowerment Seminar (YES) (for 15-18 year olds)
- The Youth Empowerment Seminar Plus (YES+) (for 18+ year olds)
- The Prison Programme
- Achieving Personal Excellence Program (APEX) *www.apexprogram.org*
- Sri Sri Yoga *www.srisriyoga.in*

The International Association for Human Values

(www.iahv.org)

The International Association for Human Values (IAHV) was founded in Geneva in 1997, to foster, on a global scale, a deeper understanding of the values that unite us as a single human community. Its vision is to celebrate distinct traditions and diversity, while simultaneously creating a greater understanding and appreciation of our many shared principles. To this end, the IAHV develops and promotes programmes that generate awareness and encourage the practice of human values in everyday life. It upholds that the incorporation of human values into all aspects of life, will ultimately lead to harmony amidst diversity, and the development of a more peaceful, just and sustainable world. The IAHV works in collaboration with partners dedicated to similar goals, including governments, multilateral agencies, educational institutions, NGOs, corporations and individuals.

Service Projects

- Sustainable Rural Development
- Organic Farming
- Trauma Relief
- Peace Initiatives
- Education (www.ssrvm.org)
- Women Empowerment
- Drug Addiction Rehabilitation

International Centres

INDIA
21st km, Kanakapura Road
Udayapura
Bangalore - 560 082
Karnataka
Telephone : 91-80-28432273, 74
Fax : 91-80-28432832
email : info@vvmvp.org

CANADA
Box 170-13 Infinity Road
St. Mathieu-du-Parc
Quebec, G0X 1N0
Telephone : 819- 532-3328
Fax : 819-532-2033
email : artofliving.northeast@sympatico.ca

GERMANY
Bad Antogast 1
77728 Oppenau
Telephone : 0049 7804-910 923
Fax : 0049 7804-910 924
email : artofliving.germany@t-online.de

• www.srisriravishankar.org • www.artofliving.org
• www.iahv.org • www.5h.org